A YEAR OF PROGRAMS FOR TEENS 2

ALA Editions purchases fund advocacy, awareness, and accreditation programs for library professionals worldwide.

A YEAR OF PROGRAMS FOR TEENS 2

Amy J. Alessio | Kimberly A. Patton

AMERICAN LIBRARY ASSOCIATION
CHICAGO   2011

Amy J. Alessio is a teen librarian at Schaumburg Township District Library in Illinois. She reviews young adult literature and mysteries for *Crimespree Magazine* and Teen reads.com and writes and edits fiction and nonfiction, including *A Year of Programs for Teens* (2006), which she coauthored with Kim Patton. Amy served two terms on the Young Adult Library Services Association board of directors, and she was honored in 2006 with the Illinois Library Association's Davis Cup Award for librarians serving youth. Amy is also passionate about cookbooks; she presents programs about them and writes about them in her Vintage Cookbooks and Crafts blog and on her website, www.amyalessio.com.

Kimberly A. Patton is teen librarian at the Kansas City Public Library Central Resource Branch in Kansas City, Missouri. Before moving to Kansas City, she served as young adult specialist at the Lawrence (Kansas) Public Library. She graduated from Baker University with a BA in business administration and an MS in management. She is currently pursuing her MS in library and information science from Florida State University. Kimberly was a 2007 Spectrum Scholar and 2010 president of the Young Adult Library Services Association. She enjoys reading and cooking lavish meals for her family.

Printed in the United States of America
15 14 13 12 11   5 4 3 2 1

While extensive effort has gone into ensuring the reliability of the information in this book, the publisher makes no warranty, express or implied, with respect to the material contained herein.

ISBNs: 978-0-8389-1051-1 (paper); 978-0-8389-9308-8 (PDF). For more information on digital formats, visit the ALA Store at alastore.ala.org and select eEditions.

Library of Congress Cataloging-in-Publication Data
Alessio, Amy J.
  A year of programs for teens 2 / Amy J. Alessio and Kimberly A. Patton.
    p. cm.
  Includes bibliographical references and index.
  ISBN 978-0-8389-1051-1 (alk. paper)
  1. Young adults' libraries—Activity programs—United States. 2. Libraries and teenagers—United States. 3. Teenagers—Books and reading—United States. I. Patton, Kimberly A. II. Title.
  Z718.5.A443 2010
  027.62'6--dc22

                                        2010013661

Book design in Museo Sans and Cambria by Casey Bayer.

♾ This paper meets the requirements of ANSI/NISO Z39.48-1992 (Permanence of Paper).

Contents

PREFACE..vii

PART I CORE PROGRAMMING

1 CRAZY FOR CLUBS..**3**
What Makes a Teen Club Work?...3
What Happens When a Teen Club Does Not Work?.........................4
Developing Themed Clubs..5
CREATEens..5
Volunteering and Community Partnerships..............................7
Money Mavericks..8
Techno Teens..10
Drama Dynamics..11
Telling Stories with Film...12

2 REALLY POPULAR READING PROGRAMS..............................**15**
What Is the Goal of the Reading Program?............................15
What Happens When a Reading Program Does Not Work?..................16
Take It Easy (on Teens and on Staff!)...............................17
Summer and Winter Reading Promotions................................17
Year-Round Reading Programs...19

3 COLLECTION CONNECTION..**21**
Mystery Madness...22
Heartbreakers...23
Vamping It Up...24
Short but Not Sweet: Novels under 200 Pages.........................26
Inspired Reads: Christian Fiction...................................27
Spending Savvy..28
Romance in This Life and Beyond.....................................29
Art of Reading..30
Super Science...31
Fabulous Food: Fiction and Nonfiction...............................32

4 PUZZLES AND OTHER PASSIVE ACTIVITIES.........................**33**
Little-Known Library Facts: Two Truths and a Lie....................34
How Will It End?..35
Whose Team Are You On?..36
Menu Selections...37
ExerCentral...38
Holiday History...39
Vegetable Variety...40
Manga Match...41
Worst Ending in Films...42
Glamour Tools...43

PART II ANOTHER YEAR OF PROGRAMS

5 JANUARY 47

Start the Year Out Write!
"Live" Journals 48

Battle of the Best:
Book Award Programs 50

Wii Are Fit 52

6 FEBRUARY 55

Oscar-Style Teen Film Fest 56

Wild Hearts Charm Bracelets 58

Social Networking Safety Net 60

7 MARCH 63

Friendship Fest 64

March Madness Basketball and Books 66

Totally Tech Lock-in 68

8 APRIL 71

Primp Your Prom 72

Battle of the Books 74

Poetry Slam 75

9 MAY 77

Magic Moment Writing Challenge 78

Job Skills for Successful Teens 80

Summer Reading Kickoff 83

10 JUNE 85

Techno Book Discussions 86

Mystery Madness 87

Get a Clue in the Library 94

11 JULY 97

BBQ Books 98

Songwriting Contest 99

Art Media Mixer 100

12 AUGUST 103

Community Collaborations 104

Microwave Madness 106

Library Orienteering 109

13 SEPTEMBER 111

Comic Contest 112

Anime Viewers 113

Science Fair Fun: From Fabulous
Exhibits to Flops 115

14 OCTOBER 117

Totally Teen Read-in 118

Mangamania Reviewing Contest 120

Haunted Gingerbread Houses 122

15 NOVEMBER 125

Stellar Scene Contest 126

Creative Carding 127

Moneyene 129

16 DECEMBER 133

Festival of Cultures 134

Dream Rooms Design Contest 135

Decked-Out Halls 137

EPILOGUE: Wrapping It All Up 139

APPENDIX: Sample Handouts 141

INDEX 149

 Additional material available at www.alaeditions.org/webextras/.

Preface

IN THE 2006 edition of *A Year of Programs for Teens*, we presented program ideas based on several years' experience running teen events at public libraries and leading staff workshops across the country for school media specialists and public librarians.

Staff serving young adults know that keeping them coming into the school and public libraries means offering new and fresh things, or new ways of doing old favorites. In the years since publication of *A Year of Programs*, some things have changed in young adult library service. The two largest changes involve the economy and technology. At a time when fewer staff hours and less money are available for programming, social networking inspires new teen programs and offers easy ways to promote them, while rapidly changing gaming technologies prompt new services and draw in new groups of teens to enjoy them.

In *A Year of Programs for Teens 2*, we present new programs we have been involved with and offer new ideas for adapting to the shifts these economic and technological changes have wrought in school and public libraries. Part 1 features core programming. Chapter 1, "Crazy for Clubs," suggests ways to develop a variety of teen interests into regular clubs. Even as budgets are slashed, reading promotions are still a mainstay of young adult services. Chapter 2, "Really Popular Reading Program," covers a variety of such events. Booklists will always be in demand. Chapter 3, "Collection Connection," offers themed booklists on popular topics such as Vamping It Up and includes graphic novels. Staff already stretched too thin for some of the more ambitious programs can still easily reproduce the independent activities provided in chapter 4, "Puzzles and Other Passive Activities."

Part 2 provides new programs for another calendar year, complete with variations to accommodate different facilities and tips on promotion. Although the programs can be put into practice as written, they are meant as guidelines that can be customized to suit any community.

ACKNOWLEDGMENTS

The authors are grateful for the skills and patience of fabulous editor Stephanie Zvirin. We also thank agent Terry Burns from the Hartline Literary Agency for helping us with the business end of writing and the Young Adult Library Services Association for continued support and inspiration in our careers.

Part 1

Core Programming

Part 1 offers ideas for recurring events and traditional teen programming, such as monthly clubs and reading promotions. Suggestions for media lists and displays as well as puzzles are also provided to help promote teen programs or collections. Chapter 1 presents ideas for new and creative clubs that will keep teens' interests alive at your school or public library. Chapter 2 outlines plans for taking reading programs to new levels and inspiring reading events all year. In Chapter 3 readers can grab a booklist and go. The lists are also keyed to programs, making it easy to create book displays to match events. Chapter 4 features passive programs— puzzles and games teens can do in the library or online to keep their attention between events. The core programming suggested here, when combined with the special, timely programs presented in part 2, will keep teens' attention on what is new at the library each time they come in.

Crazy for Clubs

S **uccess!** A lot of teens are coming to your programs. They are clamoring for more anime or drawing or drama programs. Now what? Keep that momentum going by offering a monthly club. *A Year of Programs for Teens* outlined plans for a writing club. But there are many other ideas and themes library staff can pursue, even without specific knowledge of the topics. The key is to let the teens lead. What are they particularly interested in?

WHAT MAKES A TEEN CLUB WORK?

A successful teen club does not mean simply that the numbers of teens attending are large and increasing. For example, no one wants a huge drama group that grows each month until skits and plays become unwieldy! High attendance is a sign that the club has appeal, but it is not an appropriate gauge of success, despite what your library's administration may suggest. Success for a teen club means that teens are engaged and interested in coming each month. It means that teens are suggesting ideas for future meetings and projects. It could even mean something as simple as teens bringing ideas and techniques to a Gamers Group.

Another gauge of success could be the outcome of the group, though adults should be careful not to push the teen groups to produce. Keep in mind that the point of teen programs is to bring teens into the library and collect their feedback on improving library services for their own age group. If a volunteering group is no longer interested in helping with community or library projects, it is time to reevaluate the club and find out what other projects might hold members' interest. In any case, a teen group should not have a quota of work for the year, such as volunteering at ten projects or running ten programs or working in the youth department fifty hours this year and increasing next year. This is not their paid employment. Instead, find a gauge of success that highlights the positive outcomes: Are the club members willing to try new projects? Are they engaging with each other and not just with the friends who came in with them? Are the teens drawn together by the interest? Are they getting to know each other? Are members of themed clubs wanting to increase their knowledge of the subject? For example, has your film group suggested a film festival or expressed interest in a guest speaker?

WHAT HAPPENS WHEN A TEEN CLUB DOES NOT WORK?

Teens are teens for only four to seven years. Even a club that is active and serious about a subject may age off and fizzle out if no younger teens take up the same interest. A sign that a group is no longer working is when members are not coming up with new ideas, or when only a few come each month and just want to do a favorite social activity, such as playing board games and snacking. Although there is a place for those types of casual programs in the school or public library, they are not robust enough to be the focus of a club.

Staff should never consider permanently canceling a teen group that is not working. "I tried a teen group for a while, but no one came, so I canceled it" does not cut it with teen services. Instead, try to determine why the group is no longer relevant. For example, think of how much technology has changed in the last five years. Have your technology-related programs kept up? Are your themed clubs in tune with current teen trends? Teen services require constant feedback and adjustment.

All libraries have experienced failed teen programs, where no one comes or things do not turn out well. Clubs will change. When a club is no longer relevant, take a break from it for a few months. Circulate a survey about interests and preferred programming days and times to teens who are coming to the library. If a few teens are upset that a club has been suspended, take advantage of their interest and ask their advice in planning a new, improved one. Engage their help in volunteering in the meantime to keep them coming into the library.

When it is time to restart an old club with a new focus, or to establish a new club, spend time and effort on publicity—even more than you spend for other programs. Consider requiring applications for clubs even if all teens are automatically accepted. Having teens list their interests and reasons for coming will turn a vague interest sparked by a publicity poster into a solid commitment. Emphasize the importance of the teens' own voices in the application, such as asking teens why they want to apply to be in a particular club. This will help discourage situations where parents are forcing unwilling teens to participate. Public libraries should be sure that local schools are well informed about their programs. Having expert speakers from school staff address clubs is a good way to keep that communication going. For example, a high school art teacher could run a creative event at a meeting of the CREATEen club, described later in this chapter.

There may be times when it seems that no one is coming to teen programs, or that no one wants to come to club meetings. In such cases, try offering a virtual club, or virtual teen advisory board, with rewards for occasional face-to-face meetings. That way you can keep feedback coming in until you can recruit more teens.

DEVELOPING THEMED CLUBS

So which teen interests should staff pursue as the basis of a regular club? Let the teens decide. What was the most popular event in the summer or during the school year? Begin there. If an author event spurred teens to ask many questions about getting published, staff could likely find success with a writing club. Is college likely to be a financial hardship for many local teens? A Money Mavericks club may find interest. Does the library have more teens willing to volunteer than volunteer work for them to do? A community service club could be a great way to harness that energy.

The following are several sample themed clubs. For each, meeting and activity ideas, variations, and promotion suggestions are listed to help staff get started.

CREATEens

CREATEens is a club for teens interested in art and creative projects. Members can sample different media and ideas at each meeting, discovering new interests and talents. A library may not have enough interest from teen patrons to offer, say, a scrapbooking club, but a more general club like this can offer a session on scrapbooking and another on picture frames while yet another on collage, satisfying a wider range of interests. See chapter 11 for an outline of a standalone, mini version of this club. If you find success with that Art Media Mixer program, there is likely enough interest for CREATEens.

This club can be easy to run without hired experts, or it could be run by local art teachers and craft experts. Library staff are usually very creative people, too. Poll colleagues in other departments to see if some would be willing to present a session on knitting, beading, or other media.

Consider beginning each meeting with a slide show or samples of the featured craft from history or by professional artists. Have books and media for teens to consult while working and to take home if desired.

Activities

Clean Out the Closet Collage with Photos
Pull out items from the library craft closet and let teens be creative. Invite them to make a collage (or scrapbook page) using whatever they find—bits of wrapping paper, die-cuts, stickers and labels, ribbons and trim, and even three-dimensional items like charms. Invite teens to bring in photos for this event. They can still create collages without photos, but photo crafts are great for May and June events.

Digital Crafting
So many special printing papers and transfer items are now available for crafters. Other crafting media include digital design and color software for artists, personal die-cutting machines for creating original designs, and digital embroidery. The session might be a simple demonstration of how designs can be printed and then transferred to T-shirts or bags, or an expert could demonstrate some of the more fancy technologies for a multimedia art session.

Edible Crafts

Demonstrate different ways and ideas for decorating cupcakes or cookies with fancy frosting tips and techniques, or invite teens to create an animal or person using cupcakes or cookies. A simple candy-making session requires only a microwave, melting wafers and candy forms from the craft store, and paintbrushes for filling in detail.

Power Painting

Anyone can paint on paper. Try offering a session where teens paint a small picture or design on a variety of unusual surfaces for different effects. "Canvases" could include velvet, wood pieces, inexpensive glasses or bowls, stones, and other objects from nature. Provide permanent markers or fabric markers as additional media.

Dream Space Design

Supply or solicit bits of fabric and trims and have teens design the room of their dreams. Be sure to include some textured or furry fabrics for carpeting and furniture. Wrapping paper and photos from magazines also work well for this activity. Items can be glued onto paper in a sketch and layout of the proposed room design or used to create miniature rooms inside shoe boxes. An expert on making miniatures could take this topic even further.

Variations

- Invite teens to exhibit or sell crafts as a library fund-raiser. Or have them work on a project that is specifically intended to be sold to raise money for the library or another cause. Teens could also work on decorating a piece of art for the library, such as an outdoor bench or chairs or large pillows for the teen space.
- Teens may show so much interest in a technique or craft that a spin-off club will develop, such as a drawing club or photography club. If that happens, consider scheduling the new club at the hour right after CREATEens to maintain the audience before venturing to a new date and time.
- Offer seasonal CREATEens sessions, such as Hot Summer Crafts or Spooky Crafting.

Promotion

- Offer demonstrations of upcoming crafts at local teen centers to promote the club.
- Maintain a blog or wiki dedicated to the club with photos of samples, links to professional artists in that medium, or even small technique movies. Include photos of teens enjoying previous sessions' crafts here, too, to draw new members.
- In a display case, have the supplies, but not the finished project, and a sign inviting teens to guess what the project will be.

VOLUNTEERING AND COMMUNITY PARTNERSHIPS

S urvey teens and community agencies to identify areas where teens' help may be needed, as well as what areas teens would like to improve. Are volunteers needed for library programs? Are they needed for community events? Is there a way for the library to develop new community partnerships through a teen volunteer program? Today's teens want to improve their world; this club provides that opportunity.

Having a group that wants to slow global warming is laudable, but teens will need to see the results of their efforts to keep them coming back. How many adults remain on committees where the results of their efforts and input are never seen? Help teens take big goals and translate them into manageable projects. Consider beginning each meeting by asking teens, What can be fixed now? Consider problems in the library and in the community. Maybe the local food pantry needs birthday cake mixes and frostings for children who would otherwise not have a celebration. Maybe the shelter is desperate for personal care items. Maybe the library's teen area needs painting to cover damage. Brainstorm solutions that could be accomplished before the next meeting.

The Community Collaborations program described in chapter 12 explores some onetime partnership programs, but a volunteering club can take those ideas to the next level to provide continuous help and communication with the agencies in the area.

Activities

Creating Items of Comfort
Creating something tangible at a meeting is a quick way for teens to feel they are doing something to contribute. These activities provide momentum for bigger projects, too. For example, could the local hospital or children's shelter or even detention centers use fringed blankets made from polar fleece? Could the teens make cards for soldiers or people in nursing homes? Search online if no local agencies have such needs.

Immediate Volunteering Needs
Keep a list of events where teens are needed to volunteer and have sign-ups at each meeting. Just before the events, send e-mail to remind teens of their commitments. For the more complex events, outline what steps are needed and go through those at a meeting. For example, if teens are running the summer reading kickoff event, review times, supplies, and promotions with them and decide who will be responsible for what. Invite teens to design a reward system for volunteering to help keep them engaged. Consider a drawing for a prize, with the number of entries per teen equal to the number of hours or events for which the teen volunteered.

After Hours for a Cause
Consider hosting an after-hours program just for volunteer club members and their friends, or have the club host such an event for other teens. At the door, collect items such as food, picture books, school supplies, personal goods, or cash for the local shelter or other charitable agency or cause. The actual event could be any library program, from a gaming night to a mystery dinner to a band night.

Fund and Food Raising Fun Fair
Invite volunteer club members to run simple carnival games for families with young children. At the door, offer tickets to play the games in exchange for canned goods or

other small donations. Clean out the library closets to find old reading program prizes and trinkets to pass out as game prizes. Games could include bowling, duck pond, knocking over objects, and more.

Variations

- The Schaumburg Township District Library Teen Advisory Board ran successfully for more than ten years before breaking for six months to return at a new monthly date and time. In surveys and on applications, members told staff that they also wanted to volunteer in the library and in the community. As a result, the group became a combined teen advisory board and volunteer group called Teen Corps.
- Do local agencies have youth groups? Consider appointing volunteer club members as representatives to those groups or to local agencies such as food pantries or shelters. Each representative would be responsible for contacting a particular group, letting them know about library services and asking if the volunteer club could partner with them or help them in some way.
- Organize a drop-in event where a few teens at a time read to younger kids, or have teens visit nursing homes in pairs to read books to the residents. If a local teen agency does not have funds for video games, ask volunteer club members to set up library-owned gaming equipment at their sites for demonstrations.

Promotion

- Each time the library helps another agency, ask that agency if they would not mind helping promote the volunteer group by providing space for a poster or applications or by including a mention and links on their website.
- Place volunteer club applications in schools, park districts, malls—anyplace where teens gather.
- Online library presences should feature lists of the club's previous projects with links to short videos and pictures of teens participating. Provide downloadable applications. Consider an interactive technology, like a wiki, where teens can post comments or ideas or suggest other agencies that may need help.

MONEY MAVERICKS

Although it is doubtful that teens will come flocking into a general money management program, the subject is likely on their minds. Staff need to find out which areas of money management are most interesting to teens and how those subjects can be translated into activities. Financing for college alone could have a year of topics for a monthly club on money projects. Money Mavericks is a club that explores areas of finance relevant for teens. The topic is likely of more interest to high school–age teens, but the ideas and themes are important for younger teens to know about as well. Large or very enthusiastic attendance at a program like Moneyene, described in chapter 15, could signal enough interest to support a Money Mavericks club.

Activities

Stock Selections

At the beginning of each season or year, invite teens to select companies and "purchase" stock with $1,000 in pretend cash. Members should be encouraged to watch those stocks each week. At the beginning of each meeting, help them figure out how their stocks are doing and who is gaining the most money. Consider offering an incentive or prize for the teen who "earns" the most, or invite that teen to choose a list of stocks from which the next group will spend their pretend $1,000.

College Finance

Invite teens to select two colleges or trade schools they might attend after high school (or a big-ticket item they would like to buy, if they do not plan to attend college). Find out all the costs associated with that choice— room and board, textbooks, car insurance if the choice is a car, and so on. For each member, divide the total cost by the number of months remaining before the start of college or the major purchase. Ask members to brainstorm ideas for raising money. Introduce the subject of compound interest and explain how that can help.

Scholarship and Grant Searches

Give teens a list of local agencies that offer scholarships and provide references and computer access to help them find more. Do they know all the areas of interest for which scholarships are offered or which colleges may offer them financial help? What is the process for getting loans, and what are the long-term costs? Review these topics based on the college or big-ticket item each member chose for the College Finance activity (see above).

Savings Board

Have teens track pretend or real savings in a group blog or wiki. They can also post or discuss at meetings something they did to save money. No amount saved would be too small to give ideas to others.

Credit Caution

Give teens scenarios in which they have to make choices about spending, including whether to use credit. Ask them to act out the scenarios, and the consequences of their choices, at another meeting.

Variations

- The Money Mavericks could be a virtual club with weekly or monthly money updates. Teens would need an online forum for discussion, such as a simple website or a wiki. An e-mail discussion list could work as a start.
- Money topics are of interest to people of all ages. The library could host a series of money management programs for seniors, adults, and teens, led by local experts.
- Offer programs on evaluating and maintaining big-ticket items that appeal to teens, such as buying a first car, simple car repairs you can do yourself, testing features of the latest techno gadgets, or DIY computer upgrades.

Promotion

- Many local schools and community colleges would likely be willing to promote a money management club. Contact specific offices, such as social science departments, counseling offices and centers, and business classes.
- Promote the club to parents, including staff members with teen children. Offer summaries of the topics for each meeting.
- Display a jar of old shredded dollar bills (often available at novelty retailers) or a jar of coins next to a poster promoting the club. Invite teens to guess how much money is there.
- For online promotions of the club, announce how much money needs to be saved for a few local colleges and add a countdown widget indicating how much time is left before that money has to be paid.

TECHNO TEENS

Technology and teens are BFFs, so make the most of it by incorporating technology into as many teen programs as possible. Tech-savvy teens will appreciate the use of technology and innovation to create interactive teen programs. Adding a technology component to traditional programs will help keep them fresh for new teen patrons.

Activities

Game Night

Invite teens to play their favorite video games at the library. When selecting games yourself, be familiar with the games you are planning to use before your event. Choose a wide variety of games to cover the interests of all ages and of both boys and girls. Have teens play rounds to see who can score the highest at each level or, if you have enough gaming consoles and time, allow teams to play each other for high score. Set up game consoles and either midsized television sets or projectors and screens around the room to accommodate spectators. Sign teens up to play each game in the order that they arrive at the library. Some businesses will loan out gaming equipment if you allow one of their staff members to attend the event and help set up and tear down equipment. This is especially helpful if an issue arises with the equipment and you need a quick and ready expert to handle technical emergencies.

Speed Texting

Who has the fastest fingers in the West? Skip the gaming equipment entirely and use cell phones to have a great teen event. Type up a few sentences or a paragraph and have teens race against the clock and each other to see who can text it into their phone the quickest.

Ringtone Musical Chairs

Add a techno twist to traditional musical chairs by playing random ringtones instead of regular music.

Name That Ringer

Play a few bars of a popular ringtone and letting teens compete to see who can name it the soonest.

Interactive Book Club

Post book discussion questions or book-related trivia quizzes to create interactive book discussion programs and enable more teens to participate.

Variation

- Kick up the competition by challenging school branches or other libraries in your region online. You will need online capabilities, so schedule a visit with your technical staff.

Promotion

- Use the library website or social networking site to post schedules of library events for teens.
- Loan teens film and voice recording equipment so that the library's teen programs and events can be promoted in advance or broadcast live.
- Partner with local electronic gaming stores to promote the event and obtain prizes.

DRAMA DYNAMICS

Drama exercises help teens learn how to communicate more effectively. Fun creative exercises get teens to thinking outside the box and help develop storytelling skills.

Activities

Improv

Stimulate creative thinking presentation skills with a fun and energizing improvisational acting activity. Invite a local drama teacher to share acting techniques involving emotions, using facial expressions, mime, and movement. Challenge teams to act out one-line scenes written in advance and pulled out of a hat. Or have participants divide into groups and create their own story with unique plots and characters and act them out for the audience.

Promotional Film

Create a script to promote the library or teen events. Have one group of teens choose props, create costumes, and build sets. Have a second group act out the script while the third group films their performance. Once completed, have a premier screening at the library and invite staff, friends, family, and others in the community. Share the video with administrative staff, community leaders, and library advocates and be sure to add it to the library's website for further viewing.

Lighting and Mood Design

Invite local theater members or crew to do a demonstration of how simple lighting and props can bring a new dimension to skits. Consider having teens put together a small show or puppet theater using these techniques for younger children. Visit a local production studio through colleges or other venues so teens can see the entire process as it is put together for television.

Variations

- Ask teens for their opinions on three popular movies for best mood lighting and effects for online voting. Link also to classics or other movies they may enjoy available through the library.
- Invite teens to enter a short YouTube-style video for a reading promotion or National Library Week. Themed movies are another option.

Promotion

- Contact drama instructors from local schools and colleges and any private drama instructors in the community and invite them to participate and help promote the program. Offer to have the teens help produce a video promotion for their programs, too.
- Contact the local media outlets to alert them to the library promotion and ask them to broadcast it as a public service announcement.
- Once teens have mastered their production skills, contact social service agencies in the area that deal with teen issues and offer to have the teens help produce a video promotion for their programs, too.
- Partner with area production companies to get expert tips from their staff and invite them to send representatives to teach acting and production skills to students.

TELLING STORIES WITH FILM

Drama club teens may want to take moviemaking and editing to another level. Here is an opportunity to grow an interest into another club. Helping teens learn to tell stories in a new medium helps them learn to express themselves more effectively. Using easy-to-use software such as Windows MovieMaker, teens can combine text, videos, photos, and illustrations to make short video stories. For help in teaching storyboard and video editing techniques, contact film and drama instructors in your area.

Activities

Book Trailers

Book trailers are a great way to share book reviews and a creative alternative to written reviews. Ask members to develop scripts from written reviews and then create their own videos, or have them choose images from a public domain image site to accompany text captions taken from the review. Once the book trailers are completed, use them as booktalks or add them to the library website.

Autobiography

Ask teens to compose a short autobiography or answer a few questions about themselves and have them combine this script with video clips and photos of family and friends.

Promotional Video

Select an annual library event, such as Teen Tech Week or Teen Read Week, and ask members to use your promotional copy and the previous year's event photos and video to create a promotional video for the current year's event.

Variations

- Invite members of this group to work with the writing club or drama club members on a larger production.
- Offer a serial story or newscast in short movies on the library teen site.
- Teach teens simple animation with Animoto or the free Pencil software and build toward short cartoons to be offered on the library teen site.

Promotion

- Send the trailers to area schools and community groups to promote the club.
- Partner with community parks and recreation agencies or art centers that can provide access to more filmmaking equipment. Work out a deal where your teens create short promotional videos about their agencies that can be shown to donors, administrators, and others in the community.

2

Really Popular Reading Programs

Reading programs are typically a library's favorite events to host for teens. Even when libraries have little money for staff and programs, many will still offer teens incentives for reading in the summer. Summer reading programs are a great way to bring in all types of teens. Consider capitalizing on the popularity of your summer reading program by hosting reading events now and then throughout the school year, using some of the reading celebration events described in this chapter.

But what if summer reading is not popular among teens in your community? What if the required themes turned out to be unpopular, or what if your teens hated the community-selected book? This chapter will also explore variations on summer reading programs that may prove more successful in your community.

WHAT IS THE GOAL OF THE READING PROGRAM?

It is easy to get caught up in summer reading program details like themes, prizes, kickoff events, ending celebrations, advertising, and more. But it is important to keep in mind that the main goal of a reading program is to inspire teens to read throughout the summer, or winter, or whatever period the program runs. The secondary goal may be to introduce them to library services for teens, inspiring them to keep coming in.

There may also be a specific goal each year or for each program. One year staff may want to increase teen book circulation by a stated amount or increase the number of teens participating in the reading programs. Another year the goal may be to broaden a program's appeal to include older or younger teens. Yet another goal may be to strengthen partnerships between the public library and local schools or to create partnerships with other agencies in the community that serve teens.

The planning of summer reading programs should start with setting goals and then move forward to getting teen input on how those goals will be achieved. Some schools or public libraries have to follow state or area themes each year, but that does not necessarily have to drive the entire process. Creative teens can always find an appealing tie-in with a theme, and that can be discussed while getting their input on how summer reading will run. A program that is a huge success with teens one year may not be popular the next. Although this may seem like common sense, keeping the steps of goal setting first and teen input second will help you focus all reading programs and adjust event details to keep them relevant to current and prospective teen patrons.

WHAT HAPPENS WHEN A READING PROGRAM DOES NOT WORK?

Every library will encounter a really difficult theme or One Community/Book at least once in a while or face restrictions on how summer reading will be celebrated. Public libraries also have to promote high school and middle school summer reading selections within their own summer reading events. There are always going to be parameters when running a program in conjunction with other agencies in the community, other departments in a school, or other departments in the library, and some will be difficult to follow. The Schaumburg Township District Library, for example, covers three high schools in the area, each of which usually assigns different summer reading titles. One school specifies a couple classics per grade level. Another allows teens to choose one title from a list of thirty popular and classic fiction and nonfiction titles. A third sometimes chooses one book for the entire school to read. Given the many variables and the competition among camps and summer school for teen time, there will likely be years when teen participation in summer reading goes down.

As mentioned in chapter 1, participation statistics are not the only measure of success. Summer reading participation may have been down, but perhaps more teens participated in summer events or checked out more books. Go back to the goals you set for your summer reading program. If they were not achieved, plan adjustments to keep the program relevant and appealing. What can be changed in the next program? Perhaps the incentives are no longer appealing, or the way teens report reading is daunting for reluctant readers. Teen input is very important in these areas.

Sometimes a program can be too popular. Summer at the public library is the equivalent of the holiday season for retailers. Restocking a prize that is so popular that it runs out constantly will add another task to already busy staff. Or perhaps so many teens are coming in that none of the books on the local schools' required lists are ever available. These are possible areas for adjustment. To solve the prize shortage, consider lowering demand for individual prizes by offering a greater number of prize choices. Offering a token prize for early registration will help you to gauge more accurately the number of prizes needed for the entire summer. To ensure that required books will be available, budget funds for extra copies of those books each year. Although it may seem wasteful to purchase copies that will only be checked out for a few months one year, having those books will bring in teens (and maybe the parents or siblings who drive them) who may not otherwise visit the library. Once they realize what the library has to offer, then perhaps they will check out more items and use other services. If teens come in only to find that the library has no available copies and long hold lists, they will not return.

TAKE IT EASY (ON TEENS AND ON STAFF!)

Complicated reading programs with themes, required booklists, multiple steps calling for repeated visits to the library, and more are hard on everyone. Teens who are reluctant readers or who rarely come to the library will never attempt these. And no one wants library staff to groan at the thought of another reading program. Even the most popular program is not worthwhile if it is so complicated that staff dread serving the group it attracts.

Many libraries and schools plan events several months in advance. What seems like a good idea in the cold days of February may pan out to be very stressful in the busy summer months. Even if teen input suggests otherwise, keep the parameters of the program realistic. If you plan to completely change the way summer reading is run, it is a good idea to test some of the new features in a winter reading program first. For example, if the new summer program will require teens to turn in reviews to "buy" prizes when they had previously just turned in book logs, try out the new system in the preceding winter reading program to work out kinks and issues for staff at the public desks. A school that uses a booklist to promote summer reading may want to develop a prototype list during the school year to gauge what types of titles hold teen interest and inspire class discussion.

The sections below present a variety of reading events that school and public libraries can use to motivate teens to read. Although no program is foolproof, keeping the goal of your chosen program in mind will help you adapt the elements of these programs to your specific library settings.

SUMMER AND WINTER READING PROMOTIONS

Basic Booklogs

Old school but easy, the most basic type of reading program is to have teens maintain a personal booklog of what they have read. When they reach a certain number of books, pages, or hours, they get a prize. Some libraries try to give higher requirements for teens who read graphic novels, but putting restrictions on some types of books tells the teens who love them that those books are not good enough. That defeats the purpose of the program. A simple booklog can be a good alternative for small libraries or libraries without dedicated teen staff. It may also be a good alternative for winter reading, when teens may not have as much time to read.

A variation on this basic program uses a bingo card. Each square represents a choice of attending a program or reading a particular genre of book or magazine. Teens who complete five choices in a row get the prize. This is slightly more complicated than the basic booklog, in that staff will need lists of books in each genre mentioned to help teens make their selections, but it is a good way to include program attendance as part of the summer reading initiative.

How can staff ensure that teens actually read the titles they logged? They can't. Deterring the small percentage of people who will cheat on a library reading program is not worth the effort of changing the entire program. Being inclusive is always best.

Stepped Prizes

One drawback of the booklog system is that some teens will not even try when faced with meeting a prize requirement of reading as few as four to six books over a three-month period. A stepped prize program, offering smaller prizes at preset milestones, may be more appealing in a library with many teens in that category, while being flexible enough to suit the voracious reader.

Consider offering prizes that teens can "purchase" based on the number of book reviews they turn in. For example, one book review form could garner a candy bar. Five forms could earn a coupon for $5 off fines. Invite teens who purchase the prizes quickly to enter additional reviews for chances at periodic drawings for larger prizes. If limited prizes are available, use registration cards to keep track of which teens have purchased which prizes. Tracking purchases does require more staff cooperation, so you may want to limit your selection to just a few prizes.

Auctions

Some libraries offer auctions where teens bid on prizes with book review forms as the currency. Items for bidding can range from fun hair clips to DVDs and more. An auction is an especially good option if you have a large range of donated prizes, but each in small quantities. Holding one big event to end the summer may not be practical in an area where teens are often at camp or on vacation in the summer, but offering several small auctions or an auction in conjunction with a more traditional program could appeal to even more teens. If you prefer the idea of a single event, a virtual bidding component could allow teens to make electronic bids from any location.

Special Considerations for Winter Reading Programs

More libraries are offering winter reading programs over holiday breaks to inspire pleasure reading throughout the year. Although teens definitely have a lot going on with finals and end-of-term projects, many will have time over winter break for some reading. It is important to keep this event very simple. Any of the options listed above would work, but on a smaller scale. For example, teens could be invited to read four books from December through February for a prize, and the booklogs they turn in would qualify them for a final drawing. A simplified auction would perhaps consist of a few prizes with online bidding, or silent bidding, where teens bids would increase as they read. Anyone who signed up and read a book would receive a small prize in addition to this.

Promotion for winter reading should start well before school lets out for winter break. Let teens know the winter program is coming by announcing the dates in August, when the summer reading prizes are handed out. A simple sign-up prize, like a packet of hot chocolate mix, will encourage early sign-up.

YEAR-ROUND READING PROGRAMS

As teens' schedules become more and more hectic, it is often difficult for them to participate in seasonal library activities like summer or winter reading programs. Year-round reading programs will keep teens involved no matter when their personal free time occurs. Again, simplicity works best, especially if your library plans to continue to sponsor large seasonal (summer or winter) reading programs. One or two books per month outside of school reading are about all you can ask of most teens. Invite teens to fill out a book review form for each book read and post the reviews on your library website or in your newsletter, or put up a display showing the cover of the book and the review the reader has written. Prizes should also be kept low-key. Think in terms of what appeals to teens and what will keep them coming back to the library on a regular basis. Candy and baked goods make great prizes that teens will love. The Kansas City Public library frequently hands out library bucks, which are $1 coupons that teens can use toward the purchase of a pair of headphones or a jump drive or to rent a movie. Coupons worth $5 off fines also make nice prizes if your library charges for overdue materials. Both kinds of prizes can be made by staff without costing the library a penny. Other great inexpensive prizes can be found at area discount stores, sales bins at trendy stores like Hot Topic, or anywhere else teens like to shop.

Promotion for a year-round reading program will be ongoing. Once the details of the program are worked out, begin making contact with schools and other outlets to spread the word. Create displays with helpful reading lists and show off prizes to create a buzz. Offer an incentive for teens to sign up each month to participate.

Teen Reading Celebrations

The Young Adult Library Services Association (YALSA), a division of the American Library Association (ALA), sponsors a yearly teen reading celebration called Teen Read Week. The purpose of this yearly event is to help encourage teens to spend their free time reading just for fun. Each year YALSA chooses a theme and creates publicity posters that libraries can purchase to help promote their activities during Teen Read Week. They also feature a page on their website where libraries can sign up to participate and then share ideas about activities and reading lists.

Because Teen Read Week is always scheduled for the third week in October, it provides a good opportunity for public and school librarians to work together to provide joint programs or promote the public library's programs. It is important to remember that if the timing of Teen Read Week is not right, libraries can hold teen reading celebrations at a more convenient time for their area. Celebrations do not have to be limited to one week either. You may find it hard to schedule all of the planned activities within one week; if so, change your program to a reading celebration month and spread activities out.

Teen reading celebrations should be special so librarians should make efforts to recruit local businesses to provide publicity, sponsor prizes, and even purchase extra books. Send letters to schools and other organizations promoting the celebration and the importance of recreational reading. Go big! Decorate the library, visit schools, and make a splash so that teens are aware of the program. Additional information about YALSA Teen Read Week can be found on the YALSA website: www.ala.org/yalsa/.

Everyone Reads

Everyone Reads or One Book / One Community programs are quickly becoming a great way to share and discuss books with a large number of teens and those who read teen books. Community reads are also a great way to network with other libraries in the area. In addition, these programs can be an excellent way to create interest about teen literature in general with a new community audience.

Choosing a book that will interest such a large number of participants will be a tricky endeavor, so begin by forming a committee of interested community or library leaders who possess good knowledge of teen literature and who have a good idea of what their constituents' reading preferences are. Before the first meeting, prepare a preliminary list of titles with review sources, suggested age ranges, and other helpful information so that your committee can make the best choice. Once the title has been chosen, the work really begins.

As soon as the book is chosen, begin finding sponsors to help with the expense of purchasing copies so that everyone can read the book during the allotted time. If yours is a large community or this is a citywide event, it may be impossible to have a copy for each participant, so think of clever ways to share. One way is to purchase several paperbacks, print up labels or bookmarks announcing the event to include with each book, and leave the books throughout the community in places such as schools, specific classrooms, waiting rooms, lobbies, community centers, and the like.

The next step is to schedule a variety of book discussions throughout the community hosting the event. Invite community leaders to host these discussions. If this is a school event, invite favorite teachers, club leaders, and popular athletes to lead discussions. If this is a community event, add political leaders and other local celebrities. Spice up your discussion events by adding craft times, creative writing workshops, or other activities to add to the fun of community involvement.

Awards Celebrations

Every year worthy books are honored with awards on a local, regional, and national level. Whether you agree with the choice of winners or not, join in the fun by having your own celebrations. Create displays and booklists of additional books by winning authors or compile a list of past winners to make great bookmarks.

For additional fun, host a mock award celebration. Have a committee of teen or adult readers help decide on the criteria for the award. Will you choose the most popular or the most literary? The best book in a specific genre or format? Whatever the award, develop criteria that can be used to rate the books against each other and a list of discussion questions participants can use to decide on the winner. Don't forget to publicize your award winner. Contact local schools and media. Have participating teens write the winning author to offer congratulations for their win.

3

Collection Connection

The booklists in this chapter, based on popular genres and requests, are ideal for promoting upcoming events. Space is limited at most libraries, so include booklists to make your displays do double duty! Or post these lists online with information about upcoming programs with similar themes. Just like the programs provided in part 2, several of these lists can be matched to specific times of year. Log on to ALA Editions at www .alaeditions/webextras/ to download the lists.

Booklists work best when teens are involved in their creation or can interact with them. Online comments on a blog or a place for teens to add more favorites in a particular genre are easy options. For physical book or media displays, invite teens to add titles on a bulletin board or have teen volunteers create displays.

MYSTERY MADNESS

This list could be a display before the Mystery Madness or Get a Clue programs featured in chapter 10.

Abrahams, Peter. *Down the Rabbit Hole.* New York: HarperCollins, 2006.
Soccer-playing Ingrid Levin-Hill joins a community theater production of *Alice in Wonderland* and is caught up in a police investigation following the murder of an eccentric woman associated with the troupe. (Book 1 of the Echo Falls Mystery series)

Dowd, Siobhan. *The London Eye Mystery*. New York: David Fickling Books, 2008.
Ted, who has Asperger's syndrome, may think differently from others, but he knows that there must be clues when his cousin Salim goes up in the London Eye and never comes back down.

Ferraiolo, Jack D. *The Big Splash*. New York: Amulet Books, 2008.
Matt Stevens tries to be a private detective uncovering crime at his middle school in this funny mystery.

Grabenstein, Chris. *The Crossroads*. New York: Random House, 2008.
Eleven-year-old Zack finds secrets and mysterious people cluttering the yard of his new country home. (Book 1 of the Haunted series)

Green, John. *Paper Towns*. New York: Dutton, 2008.
Paper Towns is a compelling mystery concerning missing eighteen-year-old Margot Roth Spiegelman and her neighbor, Quentin, who searches for clues as to where she went and who she is.

Haddix, Margaret Peterson. *Found*. New York: Simon and Schuster, 2008.
Jonah and Chip try to uncover clues about their adoption until the FBI tells them to stop in this futuristic thriller. (Book 1 of the Missing series)

Henderson, Lauren. *Kiss Me Kill Me*. New York: Delacorte Press, 2008.
Scarlett's first kiss goes horribly wrong when Dan dies in her arms. When she discovers it wasn't an accident, she vows to avenge him. (Book 1 of the Scarlett Wakefield series)

Jinks, Catherine. *The Reformed Vampire Support Group*. Orlando, FL: Harcourt, 2008.
Forever-fifteen Nina finds her Vampire Support Group totally annoying. They keep each other from fanging people, but then one of their group is found staked into ashes in his bedroom.

Plum-Ucci, Carol. *The Night My Sister Went Missing*. Orlando, FL: Harcourt, 2006.
Kurt and his sister are at a forbidden pier party when a shot rings out and she disappears. A night of clues, accusations, and secrets wash ashore in this mystery for older teens.

Taylor, G. P. *The First Escape*. Wheaton, IL: Tyndale House, 2008.
This "illustra-novel" follows the adventures of psychically connected twins Saskia and Sadie. (Book 1 of the Dopple Ganger Chronicles)

HEARTBREAKERS

Love can be cruel, heartbreakingly cruel. These reads will have your teens crushing and crying and dying to read more. A display of Heartbreakers would be timely to promote the Wild Hearts Charm Bracelets program for February or in April before Primp Your Prom.

Barnholdt, Lauren. *Two-Way Street.* New York: Simon Pulse, 2007.
Jordan and Courtney are totally in love. The unlikely high school couple are planning to drive cross-country together for college orientation when Jordan meets a girl on the Internet and breaks up with Courtney. But the trip is on even if their relationship is off.

Colasanti, Susane. *Waiting for You.* New York: Viking Children's Books, 2009.
Marisa learns how to be in the Now and realizes that the love she's been waiting for has been right in front of her all along.

Collins, Suzanne. *Catching Fire.* New York: Scholastic Press, 2009.
Katniss Everdeen wins the annual Hunger Games with Peeta Mellark, but it is a victory achieved by defying the Capitol and their harsh rules. Katniss and Peeta should be happy, but there are rumors of rebellion among the subjects and Katniss and Peeta, to their horror, are the faces of that rebellion.

Godbersen, Anna. *The Luxe.* New York: HarperCollins, 2008.
Beautiful sisters Elizabeth and Diana Holland rule Manhattan's social scene but are soon caught up in a whirlwind of scandal when a family secret threatens their position. This delicious novel is the first of the exciting Luxe trilogy about five compelling teens in 1899 Manhattan, where appearance matters over everything.

Green, John. *Looking for Alaska.* New York: Dutton Books, 2005.
In a stunning debut novel, Miles "Pudge" Halter befriends some fellow boarding school students whose lives are everything but boring. Pudge falls in love with Alaska, the razor-sharp and self-destructive nucleus. But when tragedy strikes, Pudge discovers the value of loving unconditionally.

Sloan, Brian. *A Really Nice Prom Mess.* New York: Simon and Schuster, 2008.
In this dynamic debut novel, Sloan infuses a senior-year tradition with hilarity and irreverence, as a gay teenager endures a surreal, endless evening that not only turns his life upside down but lands him in an unlikely romance. On Cameron and his boyfriend's night to remember, puke in the fish tank is only the beginning.

VAMPING IT UP

Zombies may be creeping up on the scene, but nothing bites like a great vampire novel. Have your teens suck up these bloodthirsty reads. While October is always a good time for a horror display, it is likely that this theme will continue to be a popular trend for teens. Consider highlighting the Vamping It Up titles before a film fest or book discussion matching any of these titles or the theme.

Atwater-Rhodes, Amelia. *Persistence of Memory.* New York: Delacorte Press, 2008.
Diagnosed with schizophrenia as a child, sixteen-year-old Erin has spent half her life in therapy and on drugs. Now she must face the possibility of weird things in the real world, including shape-shifting friends and her "alter," a centuries-old vampire.

Caine, Rachel. *Morganville Vampires.* New York: NAL Jam, 2009.
In the college town of Morganville, vampires and humans have coexisted in (relatively) bloodless harmony . . . until the arrival of Bishop, a master vampire who threatens to put the evil back in evil undead and smash the fragile peace.

Cast, P. C., and Kristen Cast. *Marked.* New York: St. Martin's Griffin, 2007.
Zoey Redbird's adventures at vampyre finishing school take a wild and dangerous turn as loyalties are tested, shocking true intentions come to light, and an ancient evil is awakened. (Book 1 of the House of Night series)

Collins, Nancy. *Vamps.* New York: HarperTeen, 2008.
At an elite vampire prep school in Manhattan, sixteen-year-old vampire socialite Lilith seeks revenge against Cally, the new student whom Lilith holds responsible for the death of her close friend during a dispute that attracted heavily armed Van Helsings. (Book 1 of the Vamps series)

de la Cruz. Melissa. *Blue Bloods.* New York: Hyperion Books for Children, 2006.
Select teenagers from some of New York City's wealthiest and most socially prominent families learn a startling secret about their bloodlines. (Book 1 of the Blue Bloods series)

Diver, Lucienne. *Vamped.* Woodbury, MN: Flux, 2009.
After being turned into a vampire, Gina realizes that she along with many other students from her high school have become pawns in an uprising within the vampire world.

Gray, Claudia. *Evernight.* New York: HarperTeen, 2008.
Sixteen-year-old Bianca, a new girl at the sinister Evernight boarding school, finds herself drawn to another outsider, Jared, but dark forces threaten to tear them apart and destroy Bianca's entire world.

Jenkins, A. M. *Night Road.* New York: HarperTeen, 2008.
Battling his own memories and fears, Cole, an extraordinarily conscientious vampire, and Sandor, a more impulsive acquaintance, spend a few months on the road, trying to train a young man who recently joined their ranks.

Jinks, Catherine. *The Reformed Vampire Support Group.* Boston: Harcourt, 2009.
Fifteen-year-old vampire Nina has been stuck for fifty-one years in a boring support group for vampires, and nothing exciting has ever happened to them—until one of them is murdered and the others must try to solve the crime.

Mead, Richelle. *Vampire Academy.* New York: Razorbill, 2007.
Two years after a horrible incident made them run away, vampire princess Lissa and her guardian-in-training Rose are found and returned to St. Vladimir's Academy, where one focuses on mastering magic, the other on physical training, while both try to avoid the perils of gossip, cliques, gruesome pranks, and sinister plots.

Meehl, Brian. *Suck It Up.* New York: Delacorte Press, 2008.
After graduating from the International Vampire League, a scrawny, teenage vampire named Morning is given the chance to fulfill his childhood dream of becoming a superhero when he embarks on a league mission to become the first vampire to reveal his identity to humans and to demonstrate how peacefully evolved, blood-substitute-drinking vampires can use their powers to help humanity.

Noel, Alyson. *Evermore.* New York: St. Martin's Griffin, 2009.
After surviving a car crash that kills her family, grief-stricken Ever finds that she is able to hear the thoughts of those around her. At her new school, she finds Damen, who has powers as well. (Book 1 of the Immortals series)

Pauley, Kimberly. *Sucks to Be Me: The All-True Confessions of Mina Hamilton.* Renton, WA: Wizards of the Coast, 2008.
When sixteen-year-old Mina is forced to take a class to help her decide whether or not to become a vampire like her parents, she also faces a choice between her lifelong best friend and the boy she has a crush on versus new friends and possible boyfriends in her mandatory "vampire lessons."

Schreiber, Ellen. *Vampire Kisses.* New York: HarperCollins, 2009.
Raven tries to shield her younger brother from the menacing Valentine Maxwell, even as she yearns to attend the prom with her immortal love, Alexander. (Book 1 of the Vampire Kisses series. A graphic novel series with these characters is also available.)

Smith, L. J. *Vampire Diaries.* New York: HarperTeen, 2009.
After returning from the afterlife, Elena is forced to battle an ancient evil when Stefan, her vampire boyfriend, goes missing.

SHORT BUT NOT SWEET

NOVELS UNDER 200 PAGES

Featuring this fun and useful list will help busy teens with assignments, especially at the beginning of the school year. Also consider setting up a display based on this list to inspire teens before a writing contest, such as the Magic Moment Writing Challenge described in chapter 9.

Anderson, Laurie Halse. *Speak.* New York: Farrar, Straus and Giroux, 1999.
Melinda barely speaks during her freshman year because she is secretly the victim of date rape. 197 pp.

Atwater-Rhodes, Amelia. *In the Forests of the Night.* New York: Delacorte, 1999.
Atwater-Rhodes wrote this first vampire fantasy work when she was thirteen. 160 pp.

Draper, Sharon. *Tears of a Tiger.* New York: Simon Pulse, 1996.
Andy goes from happy to tragic after he is the drunk driver in an accident that kills a friend. 192 pp.

Giles, Gail. *Dead Girls Don't Write Letters.* New York: Roaring Brook Press, 2003.
In this mystery, Sunny's sister returns from an apartment fire not quite as she was. 144 pp.

Johnson, Angela. *The First Part Last.* New York: Simon and Schuster Children's Publishing, 2003.
Sixteen-year-old Bobby struggles to care for his beloved baby Feather while remembering his life leading up to her birth. 144 pp.

McDonald, Janet. *Spellbound.* New York: Farrar, Straus and Giroux, 2001.
Living in the Brooklyn projects, Raven is determined to win a college scholarship to find a better life for herself and her baby son. 144 pp.

Schreiber, Ellen. *Kissing Coffins.* New York: Katherine Tegen Books, 2005.
Goth girl Raven stands out in her small town until vampirish Alexander comes to steal her heart. 176 pp. (Book 2 of the Vampire Kisses series)

Scott, Elizabeth. *Living Dead Girl.* New York: Simon Pulse, 2008.
This chilling novel for mature teens recounts life from a kidnapped girl's point of view. 170 pp.

Trueman, Terry. *Stuck in Neutral.* New York: HarperCollins, 2000.
This compelling story is told from the point of view of Shawn, who has no muscle control due to cerebral palsy. 128 pp.

Woodson, Jackie. *If You Come Softly.* New York: Speak, 2006.
Ellie and Jeremiah wade the waters of interracial romance in an elite New York prep school. 192 pp.

INSPIRED READS

CHRISTIAN FICTION

It is of course important to feature materials representing all faiths and cultures, but you may receive requests specifically for Christian fiction from local private schools or around Christmas and Easter celebrations.

Adina, Shelley. *It's All about Us*. Brentwood, TN: Faithwords, 2008.
At Spencer Academy boarding school in San Francisco, teens struggle to balance questions of dating and teen life with God. (Book 1 in the All about Us series)

Billingsley, Reshonda Tate. *Nothing but Drama.* New York: Pocket Books, 2006.
Four girls with realistic problems from pregnancy to boyfriend issues join a church group. (Book 1 of the Good Girlz series)

Carlson, Melody. *New York Debut.* New York: Zondervan, 2009.
Six teenagers living in a New York boardinghouse run by a retired fashion icon take on New York's Spring Fashion Week. (Book 6 in the Carter House Girls series)

Dayton, Anne, and May Vanderbilt. *The Miracle Girls*. Brentwood, TN: Faithwords, 2008.
Ana Dominguez knows no one when her family moves to Half Moon Bay, California. The girls there seem to see her as an enemy, and she wonders how to find friends. (Book 1 of the Miracle Girls series)

Fabry, Chris. *Blind Spot*. Wheaton, IL: Tyndale House, 2007.
Blind Spot is the first in the RPM series for younger teens, which combines racing, God, and suspense for page-turning reads.

Jones, Jenny B. *So Not Happening.* Nashville: Thomas Nelson, 2008.
Private school New Yorker Bella suffers culture shock when she has to move to Oklahoma. But life in the small town has its own intrigue to keep things interesting. (Book 1 of the Charmed Life series)

Mangum, Erynn. *Miss Match.* Colorado Springs: Navpress, 2007.
Lauren Holbrook thinks she is meant to be a matchmaker for her friends and family, beginning with her carefree singles' pastor, Nick, and her neurotic coworker, Ruby. (Book 1 of the Lauren Holbrook series)

Samson, Lisa. *Hollywood Nobody*. Colorado Springs: Navpress, 2007.
When fifteen-year-old Scotty Dawn travels to her mother's movie sets, she thinks life will be all glamour and excitement. But she learns that she can't trust everyone. (Book 1 of the Hollywood Nobody series)

Thomas, Jacquelin. *Simply Divine*. New York: Pocket Books, 2006.
Hollywood daughter Divine can't believe she's been sent to live with her pastor uncle in Georgia. (Book 1 of the Divine series)

Viguia, Debbie. *The Spring of Candy Apples*. New York: Zondervan, 2009.
Candace works at the Zone's Candy Counter while pondering college and her changing relationship with her boyfriend. (Book 4 of the Sweet Seasons series)

SPENDING SAVVY

Your teens will have the purchasing power of Wall Street wizards in no time if you share these stories of high dollars and finance. This list goes especially well with the Money Mavericks club activities discussed in chapter 1 and could be featured in the library or online before those events. It also matches the Job Skills for Successful Teens described in chapter 9 or the Moneyene program described in chapter 15.

Booth, Coe. *Tyrell.* New York: PUSH/Scholastic, 2006.
Fifteen-year-old Tyrell, who is living in a Bronx homeless shelter with his spaced-out mother and his younger brother, tries to avoid temptation so he does not end up in jail like his father.

Cheva. Cherry. *She's So Money.* New York: HarperTeen, 2008.
Maya, a high school senior bound for Stanford University, goes against her better judgment when she and a popular but somewhat disreputable boy start a profitable schoolwide cheating ring in order to save her family's Thai restaurant, which she fears will be shut down due to her irresponsible actions.

Curtis, Christopher Paul. *Bucking the Sarge.* New York: Wendy Lamb Books, 2004.
Deeply involved in his cold and manipulative mother's shady business dealings in Flint, Michigan, fourteen-year-old Luther keeps a sense of humor while running the Happy Neighbor Group Home for Men, all the while dreaming of going to college and becoming a philosopher.

Flake, Sharon. *Money Hungry.* New York: Jump at the Sun, 2007.
All thirteen-year-old Raspberry can think of is making money so that she and her mother will never have to worry about living on the streets again.

Harrison, Lisi. *Massie.* New York: Little, Brown, 2008.
In this first book of the Clique Summer Collection series, Massie is kicked out of her exclusive riding camp. When her parents insist that she get a summer job, she becomes the highest-selling Be Pretty Cosmetics girl ever by ignoring the company's philosophy.

Hartinger, Brent. *Project Sweet Life.* New York: HarperTeen, 2009.
When their fathers insist that they get summer jobs, three fifteen-year-old friends in Tacoma, Washington, dedicate their summer vacation to fooling their parents into thinking that they are working, which proves to be even harder than having real jobs would have been.

Lynch, Chris. *The Big Game of Everything.* New York: HarperTeen, 2008.
Jock and his eccentric family spend the summer working at Grampus's golf complex, where they end up learning the rules of "The Big Game of Everything."

Sachar, Louis. *Small Steps.* New York: Delacorte Press, 2006.
Three years after being released from Camp Green Lake, Armpit is trying hard to keep his life on track, but when his old pal X-Ray shows up with a tempting plan to make some easy money scalping concert tickets, Armpit reluctantly goes along.

Vail, Rachel. *Lucky.* New York: HarperTeen, 2008.
As Phoebe and her clique of privileged girlfriends get ready to graduate from eighth grade, a financial scandal threatens her family's security—as well as Phoebe's social status—but ultimately the setback teaches her the real meaning of friendship.

ROMANCE IN THIS LIFE AND BEYOND

This list is not only for fans of the Twilight series but also those who like fantasy and all things paranormal. Just like the Heartbreakers list, this list could be used in a display to promote the Wild Hearts Charm Bracelets program described in chapter 6 or the April Primp Your Prom event described in chapter 8.

Atwater-Rhodes, Amelia. *Wolfcry.* New York: Delacorte, 2006.
   In this fourth title of her Shapeshifter series, Princess Oliza is supposed to choose a mate from either her mother's hawk people or her father's serpent people to help avoid growing political tensions. Instead, she discovers a new kind of love.

Marr, Melissa. *Wicked Lovely.* New York: Harpercollins, 2007.
   Aislinn hides her ability to see faeries until two come after her in this fantasy romance. (Book 1 in the Wicked Lovely series)

McMann, Lisa. *Wake.* New York: Simon Pulse, 2008.
   Seventeen-year-old Janie gets pulled into people's dreams. When she is pulled into classmate Cable's dreams, she finds romance and a kindred spirit. (Book 1 of the Wake series)

Noel, Alyson. *Evermore.* New York: St. Martin's Griffin, 2009.
   After surviving a car crash that kills her family, grief-stricken Ever finds that she is able to hear the thoughts of those around her. At her new school, she finds Damen, who has powers as well. This is the first title of the Immortals series.

Schreiber, Ellen. *Kissing Coffins.* New York: Katherine Tegen Books, 2005.
   Goth girl Raven stands out in her small town until vampirish Alexander comes to steal her heart in the humorous Vampire Kisses series. In this second title from the series, the romance takes off. (A graphic novel series with these characters is also available.)

Schroeder, Lisa. *I Heart You, You Haunt Me.* New York: Simon Pulse, 2008.
   Ava thinks her heart is forever broken when boyfriend Jackson dies. But then she begins to sense him.

Smith, Cynthia Leitich. *Tantalize.* Boston: Candlewick Press, 2007.
   Quincy is helping her uncle run a vampire-themed restaurant in their Texas college town when her werewolf boyfriend, Kieren, becomes a suspect in a murder.

Van Diepen, Allison. *Raven.* New York: Simon Pulse, 2009.
   Nicole falls for Zin the first time she sees him. Zin is hiding his secret—he absorbs souls of the dying. This urban fantasy romance will draw readers.

Whitcomb, Laura. *A Certain Slant of Light.* New York: Graphia Books, 2005.
   Helen, who died 130 years ago, falls in love with another teen ghost as she comes to terms with her death.

Woodson, Jacqueline. *Behind You.* New York: Speak, 2006.
   In this sequel to *If You Come Softly*, Jeremiah is dead and watching over his beloved Ellie, his friends, and their families to see how they are surviving.

ART OF READING

Get those creative juices flowing with these inspiring tales of teens with talent to share. Use these titles for a display to highlight an upcoming event for CREATEens, the club discussed in chapter 1, the Creative Carding program described in chapter 15, or even the Anime Viewers program described in chapter 13.

Bauer, Cat. *Harley's Ninth.* New York: Knopf, 2007.
   Sixteen and living with her biological father in New York City, Harley Columba prepares for the first exhibition of her paintings under a cloud of worry that she is pregnant, while a trip to her hometown brings major surprises, both good and bad.

Carlson, Melody. *What Matters Most.* Elk Grove Village, IL: Multnomah Books, 2009.
   When Maya discovers talents she never knew she had, they open many unexpected doors for her.

Franklin, Emily. *The Other Half of Me.* New York: Delacorte Press, 2007.
   Feeling out of place in her athletic family, artistic sixteen-year-old Jenny Fitzgerald, whose biological father was a sperm donor, finds her half sister through the Sibling Donor Registry and contacts her, hoping that this will finally make her feel complete.

Gipi. *Garage Band.* New York: First Second, 2007.
   Four troubled boys—Guiliano, Stefano, Alberto, and Alex—form a band. When their amp blows right before the deadline for their demo tape, the boys become desperate to replace it and land themselves in more trouble than they know how to handle.

Kephart, Beth. *House of Dance.* New York: Laura Geringer Books/HarperTeen, 2008.
   During one of her daily visits across town to visit her dying grandfather, fifteen-year-old Rosie discovers a dance studio, where she finds a way to bring her family members together.

Lockhart, E. *Dramarama.* New York: Hyperion, 2007.
   Spending their summer at Wildewood Academy, an elite boarding school for the performing arts, tests the bond between Sadye and her best friend, Demi.

Sonnenblick, Jordan. *Zen and the Art of Faking It.* New York: Scholastic Press, 2007.
   When thirteen-year-old San Lee moves to a new town and school for the umpteenth time, he is looking for a way to stand out. His knowledge of Zen Buddhism, gained in his previous school, provides the answer—and the need to quickly become a convincing Zen master.

Zarr, Sara. *Story of a Girl: A Novel.* New York: Little, Brown, 2007.
   In the three years since her father caught her in the backseat of a car with an older boy, sixteen-year-old Deanna's life at home and at school has been a nightmare, but while dreaming of escaping with her brother and his family, she discovers the power of forgiveness.

SUPER SCIENCE

Incite wonder about the scientific world with stories about science and the world beyond the imagination. This list would be timely before the Science Fair Fun program described in chapter 13 or to promote pleasure reading during Teen Read Week or Teen Tech Week.

Doctorow, Cory. *Little Brother.* New York: Tor Books, 2008.
   After being interrogated for days by the Department of Homeland Security in the aftermath of a major terrorist attack on San Francisco, seventeen-year-old Marcus, released into what is now a police state, decides to use his expertise in computer hacking to set things right.

Grant, Michael. *Gone.* New York: HarperTeen, 2008.
   In a small town on the coast of California, everyone over the age of fourteen suddenly disappears, setting up a battle between the remaining kids in town and the students from a local private school, as well as a conflict between those on both sides who have "The Power" and are able to perform supernatural feats and those who do not.

Meyer, Stephenie. *The Host.* London: Little, Brown, 2008.
   The Earth has been invaded by a species that takes over the minds of their human hosts while leaving their bodies intact, and most of humanity has succumbed. Wanderer, the invading "soul" who has been given Melanie Stryder's body, didn't expect her to refuse to relinquish possession of her mind.

Patterson, James, and Michael Ledwidge. *The Dangerous Days of Daniel X.* London: Little, Brown, 2008.
   Fifteen-year-old Daniel has followed in his parents' footsteps as the Alien Hunter, exterminating beings on The List of Alien Outlaws on Terra Firma, but when he faces his first of the top ten outlaws, the very existence of Earth and another planet are at stake.

Pearson, Mary. *The Adoration of Jenna Fox.* New York: Henry Holt, 2008.
   In the not-too-distant future, when biotechnological advances have made synthetic bodies and brains possible but illegal, a seventeen-year-old girl, recovering from a serious accident and suffering from memory lapses, learns a startling secret about her existence.

Pfeffer, Susan. *The Dead and Gone.* Boston: Harcourt Children's Books, 2008.
   After a meteor hits the moon and sets off a series of horrific climate changes, seventeen-year-old Alex Morales must take care of his sisters alone in the chaos of New York City.

Shusterman, Neal. *Unwind.* New York: Simon and Schuster Children's Publishing, 2007.
   In a future world where those between the ages of thirteen and eighteen can have their lives "unwound" and their body parts harvested for use by others, three teens go to extreme lengths to uphold their beliefs—and, perhaps, save their own lives.

Westerfeld, Scott. *The Uglies.* New York: Simon Pulse, 2005.
   In Tally's world, a sixteenth birthday brings an operation, transforming one from a repellent Ugly to an attractive Pretty. Turning Pretty is all Tally has ever wanted. Her friend Shay would rather risk life on the outside. When Shay runs away, Tally must make a terrible choice.

FABULOUS FOOD

FICTION AND NONFICTION

Food lists come in handy for all types of readers, and especially those who may be interested in a career in the food industry. Use this list for displays to promote either the May Job Skills for Successful Teens event described in chapter 9 or the August Microwave Madness program described in chapter 12.

FICTION

Cohn, Rachel. *Cupcake.* New York: Simon and Schuster, 2007.
Cyd Charisse lives in New York City and works in a café while helping her cupcake-baking brother. (Book 3 of the Cyd Charisse trilogy)

Juby, Susan. *Getting the Girl: A Guide to Private Investigation, Surveillance, and Cookery.* New York: HarperTeen, 2008.
Sherman seeks the people responsible for shunning several teen girls at his school while preparing a fancy dinner for his cooking class.

Whytock, Cherry. *My Cup Runneth Over: The Life of Angelica Cookson Potts.* New York: Simon Pulse, 2005.
This humorous British story follows the recipes and adventures of Angelica, future chef. (Book 1 of the Life of Angelica Cookson Potts series)

Zieses, Lara M. *The Sweet Life of Stella Madison.* New York: Delacorte, 2009.
Stella struggles with famous chef parents who are splitting up, writing a new food column in the local newspaper, and other teen issues.

NONFICTION

Asquith, Ros. *Yummy Stuff: Ros Asquith's Teen Cookbook: The No-Worries Guide to Cooking.* London: A and C Black, 2009.
This basic cooking guide for teens comes from across the pond.

Bijlefeld, Marjolijn. *Food and You: A Guide to Healthy Habits for Teens.* Westport, CT: Greenwood Press, 2008.
This book covers everything from eating right to exercise.

Carle, Megan, and Jill Carle. *Teens Cook: How to Cook What You Want to Eat.* Berkeley: Ten Speed Press, 2004.
Teenage sisters share tips on avoiding problems in the kitchen while making everything from basic to vegetarian to ethnic meals.

Hattori, Chihiro. *The Manga Cookbook.* Tokyo: Japanime, 2007.
Teens can learn to make simple Japanese dishes like those their favorite manga characters eat.

Krizmanic, Judy. *The Teen's Vegetarian Cookbook.* New York: Puffin, 1999.
This book is a wonderful guide for teens just learning to cook and eat vegetarian.

Stern, Sam. *The Teen Survival Cookbook.* Boston: Candlewick, 2006.
With some help from his mother, Sam presents his favorite recipes, ranging from omelets to lasagna, for many different occasions.

Puzzles and Other Passive Activities

There will be many times when staff are too busy or funds are too low to offer constant teen programming. Fill in gaps with fun puzzles and other passive activities! These are mini contests in which teens can fill out questionnaires, then turn them in. Drawing names from papers turned in for prizes can be an incentive for teens to fill out the forms, but is not necessary. Perhaps the games will just be a conversation starter or time filler for teens after school. Be sure to ask participants to supply e-mail addresses in order to receive information about upcoming events. Log on to ALA Editions at www.alaeditions.org/webextras/ to download versions of the game forms without answer keys for distribution to contestants.

LITTLE-KNOWN LIBRARY FACTS

TWO TRUTHS AND A LIE

Check out these library "facts" and circle the statement that is false.

Librarians have a master's degree in library science.
Librarians are taught how to shush noisy people in the library.
Librarians learn how to quickly look up information.

One-quarter of the people who visit most public libraries are teenagers.
One-quarter of the people who visit most public libraries read tons of books.
One-quarter of the people who visit most public libraries are between the ages of twelve and seventeen.

Audiovisual materials are materials that can be both seen and heard.
Audiovisual materials include music, movies, computer games, and anything else that is multimedia.
Audiovisual materials are both very popular at the library and often easily broken.

If you have a library card, you can reserve library materials online.
If you have a library card, you can read books online.
You can ask a library staff member to scan an entire book for you to read on your computer the night before your paper is due.

Teen Read Week is the only week of the year when teens can read for fun rather than for homework.
Teen Read Week is a special week in October during which libraries feature teen books.
Teen Read Week refers to one of many weeks this library offers special events for teens.

You can find any information you need online.
Some information is only available in reference books.
Sometimes it is fastest to find answers to questions in reference books.

This library only purchases books that adults request.
This library considers requests from patrons of all ages, including teenagers.
This library usually buys materials patrons request or helps patrons find what they need through interlibrary loan.

If you damage a part of an item, like one DVD from a set, you must replace the entire set.
If you damage a library item, you may never return to the library.
If you damage an item from the library, you should report it as you realize it.

Volunteering at the library is a great way to learn about the services you can use.
Volunteering at the library is boring.
Volunteering at the library may help you in the future when you apply for paid employment.

Teens are not allowed to read books from the youth or adult sections.
Teens are allowed to read books from any section of the library, per their parents' guidance.
Teens are allowed to read fiction, nonfiction, and graphic novels.

HOW WILL IT END?

Do you sometimes hate the endings of books or movies? Now it's your chance to write a great one! Create an ending (no more than 500 words) to one of these scenarios.

SCENARIO 1

Ashley and Amber have been friends since preschool, but now Amber seems to want to spend time with her new high school sports crowd. Ashley heard that Amber was talking about her and is ready to tell her off and never speak to her again. She is waiting for Amber in front of the school after tennis practice to do just that. *What happens when Ashley confronts Amber?*

_____

_____

_____

_____

SCENARIO 2

Practically the moment he turned sixteen, Steve applied for a paid position as assistant coach at the local kiddie sports group. He had played with the group for years as a kid, then volunteered as a teen. He is told that the positions are not being filled because funding is running out. He really needs money to save for college. *What happens next for Steve?*

_____

_____

_____

_____

SCENARIO 3

Rachel enjoyed going out on a few group dates where she was paired with Kel. She is stunned when he sends her a text telling her to leave him alone. His friend Jake told her Kel was also making fun of her. She is ready to confront Kel at a party that she and her friends will be attending. *What will happen at the party?*

_____

_____

_____

_____

WHOSE TEAM ARE YOU ON?

Team Edward or Team Jacob? Team Peeta or Team Gale? Which team would you choose in these character matchups? Choose one of the following books or series and write a brief paragraph telling us who your favorite character is and why.

TEAM EDWARD OR TEAM JACOB?
Twilight series by Stephenie Meyer

_____

_____

TEAM PEETA OR TEAM GALE?
The Hunger Games by Suzanne Collins

_____

_____

TEAM MASSIE OR TEAM ALICIA?
The Clique series by Lisi Harrison

_____

_____

TEAM BUFFY OR TEAM SOOKIE?
Buffy the Vampire Slayer series (various authors) and *Sookie Stackhouse Stories* by Charmaine Harris

_____

_____

TEAM SERENA OR TEAM BLAIR?
Gossip Girl series by Cicely von Ziegesar

_____

_____

TEAM KAROLINA OR TEAM NICO?
Runaways by Brian K. Vaughan

_____

_____

TEAM TITANS OR TEAM X MEN?
New Teen Titans series (various authors) and Uncanny X Men series (various authors)

_____

_____

TEAM ALEX OR TEAM MAX?
Alex Rider series by Anthony Horowitz and Maximum Ride series by James Patterson

_____

_____

MENU SELECTIONS

Can you pick the healthiest choice from a menu? Rank these restaurant favorites in the order from 1 to 10, lowest calories to highest, and see if you are correct.

____ Fast-food hamburger

____ 12-inch meatball submarine sandwich

____ 8-inch personal pepperoni pizza

____ Large order of curly fries

____ Tuna fish sandwich

____ Four-piece serving of chicken nuggets

____ Taco salad with tortilla chips

____ Fast-food burrito

____ Four mozzarella sticks

____ Side of macaroni and cheese

ANSWERS

1. chicken nuggets: 170 calories (90 from fat); 2. macaroni and cheese: 180 calories (80 from fat); 3. hamburger: 250 calories (80 from fat); 4. beef burrito: 410 calories (240 from fat); 5. mozzarella sticks: 425 calories (254 from fat); 6. curly fries: 480 calories (210 from fat); 7. taco salad with tortilla chips: 580 calories (270 from fat); 8. pepperoni pizza: 790 calories (290 from fat); 9. tuna fish sandwich: 1,060 calories (560 from fat); 10. meatball sandwich: 1,120 calories (440 from fat).

Correct answers are based on calorie counts listed on The Fast Food Explorer at www.fatcalories.com. Results may vary across different restaurants.

EXERCENTRAL

Do you know how many calories you really burn with Wii Fit? Does bowling count as exercise? Rank the following activities from 1 to 10, lowest burn to highest.

____ Fast walking

____ Wii Fit Yoga Training

____ Hiking

____ Tae kwon do

____ Stationary bike

____ Wii Sports Tennis

____ Bowling

____ Rollerblading

____ Swimming laps

____ Basketball game

ANSWERS

1. Wii Fit Yoga Training (175 cal/hr); 2. bowling (219 cal/hr); 3. fast walking (77 cal/hr); 4. Wii Sports Tennis (341 cal/hr); 5. hiking (438 cal/hr); 6. swimming laps (511 cal/hr); 7. basketball game (584 cal/hr); 8. stationary bike (600 cal/hr); 9. tae kwon do (730 cal/hr); 10. rollerblading (913 cal/hr).

The correct answers correspond to estimates by the Mayo Clinic (www.mayoclinic.com) for a person weighing 160 pounds participating in the specific exercise for 1 hour.

HOLIDAY HISTORY

How much do you know about the most special days of the year?

1. Who was the mischievous winged child who has become associated with Valentine's Day because his arrows pierce the hearts of his victims, causing them to fall deeply in love?

   _____

2. What were the names of the two live turkeys President George Bush received in 2003, as voted on by the American public?

   _____

3. What is the name of the Grinch's dog?

   _____

4. Which NFL team traditionally hosts an annual Thanksgiving Day game?

   _____

5. In the movie *A Christmas Story*, what does Ralphie want for Christmas more than anything else in the world?

   _____

6. What is the most popular meal served on St. Patrick's Day?

   _____

7. What potato dish is served during Hanukkah?

   _____

8. Where does the name *Halloween* come from?

   _____

9. Why do New Year's revelers use noisemakers and fireworks for the festivities?

   _____

10. The Easter Bunny's visit is based on what?

    _____

ANSWERS

1. Cupid; 2. Stars and Stripes; 3. Max; 4. Dallas Cowboys; 5. BB gun; 6. corned beef and cabbage; 7. potato latkes; 8. Scotland; 9. According to tradition, to keep away evil spirits; 10. a German fable about coloring eggs so they could be identified in case of famine.

VEGETABLE VARIETY

Are you eating your five helpings a day of fruits and vegetables? Are you getting bored with baby carrots? Check to see if you know what all these vegetables are! Write the name of the vegetable pictured.

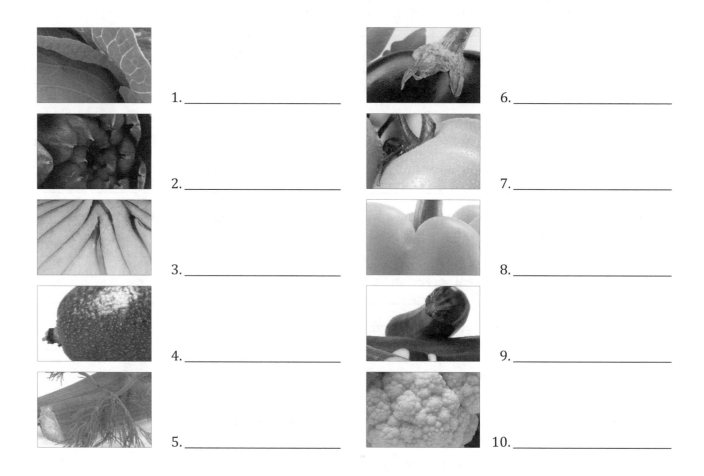

1._____

2._____

3._____

4._____

5._____

6._____

7._____

8._____

9._____

10._____

MANGA MATCH

Think you know your manga characters? Match these books with the popular characters they feature.

1. *Hack*

2. *Harlem Beat*

3. *Kara Kano*

4. *One Piece*

5. *PhD Phantasy Degree*

6. *The Rain Goddess*

7. *Astro Boy*

8. *Ghost in the Shell*

9. *After School Nightmare*

10. *Death Note*

A. Mashiro Ichijo

B. Monkey D. Luffy

C. Shugo and Rena

D. Kira

E. Sang

F. Toby

G. Yukina and Soichiro

H. Gimmy

I. Nate Torres

J. Motoko Kusanagi

WORST ENDING IN FILMS

Ever hate the ending of a movie? Think writing a screenplay is easy? Choose a movie from the list below (or think of your own worst-ending film), then write the ending it should have had.

Indiana Jones and the Kingdom of the Crystal Skull

War of the Worlds

The Blair Witch Project

The Lord of the Rings: The Return of the King

Grease

Signs

The Sixth Sense

Planet of the Apes

King Kong

Old Yeller

Pirates of the Caribbean: Dead Man's Chest

I Am Legend

_____

_____

_____

_____

_____

_____

_____

_____

_____

_____

_____

_____

GLAMOUR TOOLS

What on earth do these things do? Write the names or functions of the glamour tools pictured.

1. _____

2. _____

3. _____

4. _____

5. _____

6. _____

7. _____

8. _____

9. _____

10. _____

Another Year of Programs

In the second part of this book, program suggestions are arranged by the calendar year for planning. It is of course entirely possible to offer many of these at different times. The Variations section provided for each event gives some tips for that as well. Programs are broken down into fairly standardized steps and topics to make them easier to follow and execute:

- **Preparation Time.** This refers to how much time the authors feel should be allowed to publicize and prepare for the event. Two months is most often given as a guideline. This does not mean that an entire two months will be spent promoting a Magic Moment Writing Challenge, for example, just that publicity should start two months before at least.

- **Length of Program.** Contests usually run for one week to one month, but most events run one to two hours. This is meant as a guideline based on the authors' experiences.

- **Number of Teens.** Again, this will vary by facility, but attendance numbers set by the authors indicate limits beyond which an event may be unmanageable.

- **Suggested Age Range.** The authors have chosen ranges of teens to match their experience to the appeal for a particular event and may include tips on how to expand the program for older or younger teens.

- **Shopping List.** There is nothing worse than planning for a program and forgetting something crucial, like prizes for a contest or ingredients for cooking. The Shopping List section is meant as a guideline of basic needs to run that described event. It is possible to offer a contest with simple ribbon prizes and still have a successful event without expensive prizes. Teens at different facilities may have different expectations and limitations.

- **Set It Up.** This section outlines what will happen prior to the event, from publicizing to setting up rooms.

- **Make It Happen.** This section provides the step of the event, in order.

- **Variations.** Variations make the program possible for different-sized facilities or out in the community. This section also lists ways to grow the program if there is a lot of interest or new things to try if there is little interest.

- **Promotion.** What are some targeted ways to promote this particular program? This section offers unique ideas for marketing each event.

January

January is a tough time to get teens into programs. Many winter sports start up during this month, and finals and semester-end activities take time and attention from high school teens. Younger teens may not have finals to worry about, but they may be tired of being trapped inside with bad weather and are looking for something to do. Older teens also may need to let off some steam.

Focus on starting off the New Year with healthy and creative programs. It is best to have low-maintenance or drop-in events at this time because of the competition for teen attention, but it is still possible to have quality programs.

The beginning of a calendar year is the perfect time to highlight journaling and writing. In Start the Year Out Write! teens will explore ways to express themselves both on the outside of a journal and on the inside. Battle of the Best is designed to encourage excitement about the library literature awards for teens, as those announcements are made in January also. Wii Are Fit features healthy habits, another great New Year's resolution. New and easy games and snack preparation make feeling good even easier for busy teens.

Winter reading programs may still be engaging teen readers this month. So even for a month that is very busy for teens, there are plenty of possible programs that offer support and entertainment.

START THE YEAR OUT WRITE!

"LIVE" JOURNALS

These cool journals are called "live" because they are covered in animal print and fake fur! Encourage teens to develop the healthy habit of regular journal writing by helping them to create a cool place of their own to jot down their thoughts.

Whether writing a journal by hand or using an online site, your teens can get the most out of their journaling experience when you share these tips. First of all, there are no specific rules to keeping a journal. It's private, it's personal, and everyone's is different. Teens may write in whatever style they choose. Some prefer to keep a traditional daily journal, some weekly; others write only in verse; others keep a journal about places they visit or interesting people they meet. It helps teens develop a consistent journaling habit if they stick to a comfortable space and time of day to write. Encourage teens to express themselves by using colored pens and stickers, cutting words out of magazines, and varying fonts and font sizes. Above all, make it fun!

PREPARATION TIME

60 minutes

LENGTH OF PROGRAM

12-hour drop-in format

NUMBER OF TEENS

20–25

SUGGESTED AGE RANGE

Grades 6–12

SHOPPING LIST

- ❑ 20–25 notebooks of various sizes and shapes
- ❑ Markers, pens
- ❑ Fabric pens and fabric paint
- ❑ Fabric and felt pieces in a variety of patterns and sizes
- ❑ Fake fur and animal prints
- ❑ Googly eyes in various shapes
- ❑ Stickers
- ❑ Glue
- ❑ Glitter
- ❑ Finger foods are good for writing and can consist of a vegetable tray and dip, chips, pretzels, cookies, and coffee, tea and cocoa to drink
- ❑ Music and a portable CD player (background music to help foster a writing mood)

SET IT UP

TWO WEEKS BEFORE

The first part of the year is the perfect time to begin keeping a journal! Make sure to begin announcing this program with all of your year-end announcements in December, just before the end of the semester. Include flyers and information on all programming calendars and holiday event guides.

DAY OF PROGRAM

In a designated meeting room or section of the library where teens are allowed to spread out their craft supplies, listen to music and enjoy the snacks provided. Prep your animal print fabric and fake fur by measuring and cutting pieces to cover your notebooks. Make a sample journal complete with writing prompts as an example.

MAKE IT HAPPEN

1. Once all the prep work is finished, this program practically runs itself. Set up all the craft materials and let teens choose the supplies they would like to use to decorate their journals. Provide a list of journal prompts for them to place in their journals to be used as instant writing ideas. Play some teen-friendly background music to provide a creative, relaxed atmosphere. Let teens "go wild" with their own ideas for their journals.

2. Consider offering simple drinks or snacks for this event. Coffees, teas, and hot chocolate will make this a cozy winter activity. Finger foods such as fresh fruits and veggies along with cookies or cupcakes will make the perfect type of snack for this activity.

VARIATIONS

This kind of program can easily be offered as on online program. Teens may either explore sites like LiveJournal to set up online journals or use word processing programs to set up templates. They may not be as concerned and stressed about time and may be looking for something to do.

PROMOTION

Advertising ahead of time can be done at the schools before the end of the previous semester and holiday break. Send fun flyers to school media centers and have school personnel make announcements over the PA system. Consider partnering with English and/or creative writing instructors for guidance or extra-credit opportunities for teens attending your event.

BATTLE OF THE BEST

BOOK AWARD PROGRAMS

January is book award season, so plan ahead and examine the lists of nominated titles to have a heads-up on the announcements. A good way to get teens in the spirit is by having a Battle of the Book Award Winners contest. Catching up on past winners and the qualifications for each award will help teens be more discriminating in their reading styles. By looking through the judges' eyes, they can get a glimpse of all the considerations that go into choosing a winning title from all the many books written each year. Teens will also get a feel of how each committee is different and how winning titles vary from year to year.

PREPARATION TIME

Approximately 2 weeks

LENGTH OF PROGRAM

2–4 weeks

NUMBER OF TEENS

10–50

SUGGESTED AGE RANGE

Grades 6–10

SHOPPING LIST

- ❑ Gift certificates and coupons for prizes
- ❑ 4 buzzers or egg timers for the trivia game
- ❑ Pens and pencils
- ❑ Name tags
- ❑ Donated items for door prizes and giveaways
- ❑ Cookies
- ❑ Punch
- ❑ Ice
- ❑ Tablecloths, napkins, plates, cups

Note: Refreshments and supplies will cost about $50 (per 50 attendees).

SET IT UP

ONE MONTH BEFORE

Decide which awards books or authors you want to battle. Choices include: Printz Award winners and honors; Best Books for Young Adults or Quick Picks Top Tens; Alex Awards books; Margaret A. Edwards Award–winning authors; or any other notable or award-winning books you would like to use. Prepare a Battle of the Best reading list and reading log with space for titles, authors, and reviews. In addition, prepare a list of discussion questions for each title to be read, making sure to include the question, the passage it refers to, and the page the passage can be found on. Prepare lists of books and trivia questions. Set out publicity as early as possible, including book displays and bookmarks, to get teens reading the featured books.

Contact area businesses and solicit donations for prizes or begin shopping for prizes to give to teens who read all the titles, participate in the trivia battle, or win the challenge either individually or on a team, depending on how you host the event.

MAKE IT HAPPEN

1. Set up refreshments and tables with chairs for trivia game participants. Invite a teen to be emcee, or have staff perform that function. If teens are not in teams, keep track of how many are participating and what to do if two raise their hands at the same time. Some sort of tiebreaker will be needed for teams as well.

2. Set up timers on some tables for final and bonus rounds. Keep the total of books to be read rather small (less than ten is best).

3. Prizes and promotions need not be elaborate or expensive. Solicit donations, discounts, and prizes from area merchants. Use leftover summer reading or Teen Read Week coupons and prizes.

VARIATIONS

- Have a variety of different-sized prizes; give everyone a small prize, like a free hot chocolate, then give larger prizes to those who do well in the trivia contest.
- Partner with school or public libraries in the area to promote the program; consider forming teams to challenge each other.
- Instead of trivia questions and answers, set up a PowerPoint *Jeopardy-* or *Who Wants to Be a Millionaire*–style game.

PROMOTION

Decorate the library with a championship theme using blue ribbons, trophies, medals, etc., as props. Tape or glue the covers of the featured books on the props to decorate the room. Put the featured titles on display and make trivia bookmarks for each book. Make flyers with all the information about the event and share them with schools, libraries, and other agencies in the area.

Wii ARE FIT

Being healthy is especially important for growing teens, and there are fun and simple ways to promote this through a drop-in event. An afternoon fitness sampler with stations and activities should entice lots of teens to try exercising.

PREPARATION TIME

2 months

LENGTH OF PROGRAM

3 hours

NUMBER OF TEENS

30–50

SUGGESTED AGE RANGE

Grades 6–10

SHOPPING LIST

- ❑ Make your own trail mix: dried fruits, nuts, granola, cereal, carob chips, or M&Ms (tiny ones)
- ❑ Granola bars, oatmeal cookies, assorted fruit
- ❑ Juice or Gatorade
- ❑ Gaming equipment, including
    - ❑ 2 Wii platforms (minimum)
    - ❑ Wii Balance Board and Wii Fit game
    - ❑ Dance Dance Revolution game and dance pads
    - ❑ Screens
- ❑ Video equipment
    - ❑ DVD player
- ❑ Instructional DVDs, such as
    - ❑ Martial arts
    - ❑ Step aerobics
    - ❑ Yoga
- ❑ 3 to 5 steppers
- ❑ 5 Hula-Hoops
- ❑ 5 jump ropes
- ❑ Yoga mats
- ❑ Counters for contests
- ❑ Resistance bands
- ❑ Swiss balls in a variety of sizes

SET IT UP

ONE MONTH BEFORE

- Become familiar with some video game exercise media, including Wii Fit, Dance Dance Revolution (DDR), We Ski, Active Life Outdoor Challenge, or My Fitness Coach.
- Choose instructional DVDs on simple martial arts, yoga, or step aerobics, or contact local folks who may be willing to teach those forms of exercise.
- Look up simple exercises for resistance bands and Swiss balls and print out instructions. Or, again, find a local physical therapist or trainer to assist with that station.
- Plan a schedule for the event to allow teens to alternate times for each station. Hold mini contests on activities like DDR, jump roping, and Hula-Hooping.

DAY OF PROGRAM

Set up stations around the room, including private Wii Fit and screen for teens who want to take the body fitness assessment provided in that game. Players who want to try Wii Fit must go through this process and teens will be self-conscious about weight and fitness.

MAKE IT HAPPEN

1. When teens arrive, direct them to a station. Encourage them to try simple stretching exercises and not overdo it at any one activity. Teens could be limited to a certain amount of time if necessary at each station for crowd control.

2. Stations may include: Make Your Own Trail Mix, Wii Fitness Assessment, DDR, Resistance Bands and Swiss Balls, Jump Rope and Hula-Hoop, My Fitness Coach (or other active Wii game with another balance board), Step Aerobics with DVD.

3. On every half hour, hold a mini contest with prizes like water bottles and pedometers. These contests could include: how many jump rope revolutions per minute, who can jump rope the longest, who can hula the longest or the most revolutions, DDR scores. On every hour, present a mini demonstration of a new exercise. Teens may choose to stay in stations, but the demonstration can go on in the middle of the room; for example, yoga stretching or power stepping or martial arts.

4. New versions and activities for the Wii Fit and Balance Board are being released often. The Wii Fit Plus allows more than one player to switch off during activities and introduces several new exercises, including snowball fights and rhythmic kung fu. Some of the games require more paraphernalia; it may be fun to have a station where teens could try them out at least briefly or see a demonstration.

VARIATIONS

- Offer a series of smaller programs exploring different forms of exercise. For example, one week may highlight aerobics, the next Pilates, the next martial arts. At each program, a different healthy snack could be featured. Teens who come to at least four of the series would get a prize, which could be a gift certificate to the YMCA or local gym.
- Work with the local park district or YMCA on this program and include exercise at their facilities, including swimming or rock climbing.

PROMOTION

- Set up exercise demos at teen programs in the weeks ahead so teens get a feel for what will happen at the main event. This could include mini jump rope contests in the teen area—perfect for settling the after-school crowd!
- Contact local gyms and community organizations to help advertise the event.

February

February is a great month for programs at the library. There is so much going on. Food themes are great for Valentine's Day, while Black History Month and Lincoln's birthday provide forums for speakers, displays, and interactive educational experiences. Many libraries are already honoring these important occasions. In this book, some different yet timely ideas are offered to supplement such events.

The weather is still cold outside in many areas, so an Oscar-Style Teen Film Fest may be just the ticket to bring teens into the library. No expensive gown and jewelry required! Wild Hearts Charm Bracelets is a craft class that is timely for Valentine's Day yet general enough to match with great girl books. The Social Networking Safety Net is also a good winter program because lots of teens stay inside on their computers. Variations of this one can be offered for teens or parents, or even online, to help families utilize the best of these technologies in a safe manner.

OSCAR-STYLE TEEN FILM FEST

Oscar buzz is everywhere this time of year. Why not capture the interest of teens by having them host their own teen film festival? Movies, teens, and technology fit together so seamlessly that this is a perfect program for this time of year.

PREPARATION TIME

1 month

LENGTH OF PROGRAM

3–4 hours

NUMBER OF TEENS

100

SUGGESTED AGE RANGE

Grades 6–12

SHOPPING LIST

- ❑ Popcorn
- ❑ Pizza (donated or purchased)
- ❑ Beverages
- ❑ Tableware
- ❑ Score sheets
- ❑ DVD players
- ❑ Projectors
- ❑ Screens
- ❑ Prizes (either donated or purchased)

SET IT UP

TWO MONTHS BEFORE

Choose a theme for your festival if you are going to have an overall theme. One possibility is "Teens in the Library." Decide on the categories that will be judged. Possibilities include best short film (three minutes or less); best animated film; best screenwriting; best overall film; people's choice. Get the word out to area schools that the library is hosting a teen film festival; partner with schools, art institutes, and museums. Contact the local television stations in your area to inquire about having winning films aired.

ONE MONTH BEFORE

Contact local pizza parlors in your area and solicit donations of pizza for your event. Check in with any teens who have signed up and any community partners you have for your event. Contact local businesses for prize donations.

Once you have your theme and judging categories, make a ballot that you will print off for each teen to score the films viewed.

Set up projectors, DVD players, and screens. Use one for viewing and if possible have the other set up and ready as a backup. Pop popcorn and have it ready to serve. Set up a table for pizza and beverages. Have ballots and pencils ready to hand to teens as they enter. Have submitted films sorted by judging category and ready to view.

MAKE IT HAPPEN

1. Have teens submit final film projects two weeks in advance so that you have time to preview them and take care of any technical issues that may arise with them.

2. Set up the room for viewing the films.

3. Have prizes sorted and ready to hand out.

4. As teens arrive, pass out ballots, popcorn, and beverages. View films by categories and have teens vote after all films in each category have been viewed.

5. Allow teens to listen to music, mingle, or munch on pizza and other snacks while you tally the votes for each category.

6. At the end of the program, announce the winners.

Popcorn is a must! Soda or other beverages should be served. Pizza can be served as teens are waiting for ballots to be tallied.

VARIATIONS

- Have teens post and submit their films on YouTube.
- Use your community resources; invite a professional filmmaker to provide a program and give tips to teen filmmakers.
- Use this program as free advertisement for your library and have teens make a film about the library and their favorite service or staff person.
- Or completely skip the filmmaking aspect and choose films to view and vote on.

PROMOTION

- Advertising ahead of time can be done at the schools before the end of the previous semester and holiday break.
- Send fun flyers to school media centers and have school personnel make announcements over the PA system.
- Consider partnering with school film study instructors and others in the community to help spread the word.
- Create movie posters of teens and submitted movie titles for decorations.

WILD HEARTS CHARM BRACELETS

Charm bracelets are a sentimental sign of friendship—and what says love more than a handmade gift from the heart? These charming little bracelets can be made in numerous ways and are sure to please everyone.

PREPARATION TIME

2 weeks

LENGTH OF PROGRAM

1 hour

NUMBER OF TEENS

25

SUGGESTED AGE RANGE

Grades 6–12

SHOPPING LIST

- ❑ Ultrawhite Shrinky Dink plastic
- ❑ Hemp rope or link chains (one for each participant)
- ❑ Digital pictures of animals
- ❑ Heart-shaped charms
- ❑ Assorted beads
- ❑ Jump ring sets (one set for each participant)
- ❑ Toggle clasp set (one set for each participant)
- ❑ Eye pins
- ❑ Wire cutters
- ❑ Needle-nosed pliers
- ❑ Oven
- ❑ Pink and white cake frosting
- ❑ Sprinkles
- ❑ Cherry 7-Up and punch-flavored Kool-Aid
- ❑ Undecorated sugar cookies

SET IT UP

ONE WEEK BEFORE

Print a selection of small charm-sized pictures of various animals, insects, flowers, etc., so that teens can cut them out and make their Shrinky Dink charms.

Plan for snacks by mixing up pink and white frosting and making punch by combining Kool-Aid and Cherry 7-Up. Set out supplies and tools. Preheat the oven according to the instructions on the Shrinky Dink package.

MAKE IT HAPPEN

1. Have teens choose printed animal pictures and attach them to the Shrinky Dink sheets as described on the package.

2. Arrange them on a cookie sheet and have an adult bake them as instructed.

3. In the meantime, have teens choose the charms and beads they would like to use for their bracelets and begin putting them together. Make sure to leave a space to add the Shrinky Dink charms when they are finished baking and cooling off.

4. While waiting for the Shrinky Dink charms to cool, have teens decorate their own sugar cookie to eat.

5. After the Shrinky Dinks have been added to the bracelets, have the teens add the toggle and clasp.

VARIATIONS

- Skip making Shrinky Dinks and just use various charms and beads. Use vintage buttons or beads for a more elegant touch. Instead of purchasing chains or hemp rope, have teens make a paper clip chain.
- Decorate your own sugar cookie and serve with Bleeding Heart Punch.

PROMOTION

Pair this project with a Valentine's Day theme or use this as a craft for a Twilight-themed program. Decorate the room with snowflake hearts, hanging from paper clip chains.

SOCIAL NETWORKING SAFETY NET

M any parents of young teens are afraid of their offspring's new, passionate involvement in social networking. What are they putting online about themselves? Some parents may be afraid of technologies they have not had a chance to try.

Try an interactive approach to help patrons based on their needs or interests. Show teens new features of networking while keeping them safe, or set up a class just for parents to try out all these technologies.

PREPARATION TIME

1 month

LENGTH OF PROGRAM

90 minutes to 2 hours

NUMBER OF TEENS

12–15

SUGGESTED AGE RANGE

Grades 6–9

SHOPPING LIST

- ❏ Computer-friendly snacks if possible: less greasy chips, pretzels, M&Ms
- ❏ Computer and projector or multiple computers with Internet for hands-on work during the program
- ❏ Optional: Gift certificates to inspire teens or parents to sign up for their respective programs, for iTunes or Best Buy or other electronics store (optional)
- ❏ Digital cameras (optional)

SET IT UP

ONE MONTH BEFORE

- Set up accounts with Animoto, Facebook, Goodreads, and any other social networking sites popular in your area. (Use generic teen services e-mail to keep things separate from your personal accounts.) Other social networking sites of possible interest to parents are listed under "Variations" below. Begin using accounts so you will have things to demonstrate at the classes for each social networking site.
- Set up a wiki on a free site like www.wetpaintcentral.com or other sites. Make a separate wiki page for each social networking site you plan to cover and begin listing features and linking to your site. Make the wiki private so only participants will have access.
- Research current Pew studies and national Internet safety sites such as www.isafe.org to gather the most recent statistics related to teens' use of social networking and Internet crime.

TWO WEEKS BEFORE

Make questions for students to find answers for on each page of the wiki. For example, for Facebook:

- How do you load multiple pictures?
- How do you find people?
- What are some groups I might enjoy?
- What if someone tries to Friend me and I don't want to accept?

ONE WEEK BEFORE

- If you are going to have a class where students can work on their computers, begin sending messages to students registered suggesting they sign up for the social networking sites you are going to cover.
- Prepare a TXT quiz about social networking sites to distribute at the program.

MAKE IT HAPPEN

1. When teens arrive, the instructor's computer and/or the teen computers should be set to the wiki site. Teens can begin reading the information in the wiki and working on a simple TXT quiz handed out as they arrive.

2. The first activity could involve taking digital pictures and uploading them into at least one computer. Teens may be able to do this from their cell phones also.

3. Invite teens to set up a simple wiki page and discuss what information should and should not be provided, including contents of pictures. Slip in some statistics about Internet crime subtly.

4. When the photos are loaded, log on to Animoto and combine them into one video. This will only be possible on the presenter's computer, but let teens choose which pictures and music to use. Ask teens how this technology could be used to promote library services.

5. Spend time talking about Facebook questions. Invite teens to discuss other social networking technologies they like, such as YouTube. Teens may also show each other their various sites.

6. Be sure to highlight online library technologies, like downloadable media and databases.

7. Go over the answers to the TXT quiz and award a small prize, if desired.

VARIATIONS

- Continue the conversation with a teen club. If teens are interested in the topics, invite them to continue corresponding and discussing on the wiki by meeting periodically to highlight a new networking site or technology, such as making a YouTube video. This could morph into an online teen advisory board.
- Offer the program for parents online. Adults can be self-conscious about their lack of knowledge; an online program allows them to explore in privacy. When parents register, obtain their e-mail addresses. Set up a wiki as for the teens' class, with questions to think about for different technologies. Also include research on how teens develop skills from those tools and tips on keeping teens safe. E-mail parents the TXT quiz also to see how many know those answers as an icebreaker. Each week, highlight a different social networking tool, such as Twitter, Facebook, YouTube—whatever is popular in a particular community or seems to cause concern. Be sure to choose some sites parents could use in their own lives also, like LinkedIn and Goodreads. Parents should be setting up their own site for each of these and answering the questions on the wiki for the week or over e-mail if they prefer. Emphasize ways teens can explore these technologies safely.

PROMOTION

Use all the social networking tools available to the library to promote this one to teens. For parents and teens, make bookmarks for the program with Internet safety tips on one side and program information on the other. Make these available near all computer terminals in the library.

7

March

In many areas, the cold weather has not yet relinquished its hold on spring, yet teens are restless from being cooped up for months.** Spring break is still likely a few weeks off, and beyond that the excitement of the end-of-school-year activities.

This is a good time of year to begin recruiting younger teens for summer activities and beyond. Consider offering appealing recreational programs that also feature library services, a goal at all times, but particularly important for the recruitment function. A Friendship Fest program may motivate a shier teen who has not yet attended a teen program to come and bring her friends. Catch the attention of all sports fans with a March Madness Basketball and Books program. Celebrate library technologies during YALSA's Teen Tech Week or anytime with a Totally Tech Lock-in. From simple to elaborate, these programs combine high-interest areas with library services for maximum appeal.

FRIENDSHIP FEST

Spring break is a fun time to have a Friendship Fest for girls, or when a popular book or movie celebrating that theme is released. Too many media outlets portray female friendship as fragile, easily broken by competition. Friends are so important for teens especially, and this program will invite teens to make things for friends and celebrate those relationships.

Included for this program are directions for several projects of varying skill levels. Some may require samples to be made ahead of time. Choose activities from the ideas based on the availability of time and supplies and invite teen volunteers to help with samples.

PREPARATION TIME

2 months for publicity and shopping

LENGTH OF PROGRAM

2 hours

NUMBER OF TEENS

25

SUGGESTED AGE RANGE

Grades 5–8

SHOPPING LIST

- ❑ Snacks, including popcorn and pretzels
- ❑ Jean purses
  Note: A sewing machine will be needed for this craft with working needles and thread.
  - ❑ several pairs of old jeans in various sizes
  - ❑ Shears
  - ❑ Trims and appliqués
  - ❑ Fabric glue
  - ❑ Belting or leather cords for straps
  - ❑ Fabric markers
- ❑ Friendship autograph scrapbooks
  - ❑ Small photo albums
  - ❑ Colored paper
  - ❑ Markers
  - ❑ Stickers
  - ❑ Die-cut paper shapes
  - ❑ Ribbons
  - ❑ Interesting items to affix to pages
  - ❑ Glue

- ❏ Friendship frames with collages
    - ❏ Small craft magnetic frame kits to paint
    - ❏ Paints and brushes
    - ❏ Magazines to cut up
    - ❏ Paper for collages
    - ❏ Trims
    - ❏ Items to affix to frames
    - ❏ Glue
- ❏ Bracelets
    - ❏ Embroidery floss
    - ❏ Seed beads
    - ❏ Bracelet loom (optional)
- ❏ Friendship mural
    - ❏ Butcher paper
    - ❏ Markers

SET IT UP

TWO MONTHS BEFORE

- Begin advertising the program using posters, flyers, and online media outlets. Advertisements for the program should invite teens to bring in photos of themselves having fun with friends. Tie in a display of books or movies featuring positive female friendships.
- Solicit staff or seek out jeans in thrift stores. Make a sample purse by cutting the legs off a pair of jeans and sewing across the bottom, then attach straps to the sides. Or sew across a few inches of the leg, leaving the pre-hemmed edge as the top of the smaller purse. Attach a strap to this also. Decorate it and use it as a display to advertise the program.
- Research autograph books with silly rhymes from the 1950s and 1960s and print examples.
- Research friendship bracelets with fancy designs and beads or make a sample one with a loom.

TWO HOURS BEFORE

Set up a station for each project so that several girls can work at the same time. Another staff member at least should be present to run the sewing machine.

MAKE IT HAPPEN

JEAN PURSES

Lots of variations for these can be found online, but it is simplest to cut the legs off a small pair of jeans and sew across the bottom. A sewing machine should also be used to attach the straps. Teens can then decorate them. Or cut the bottoms of the legs off and use the hem as the top edge of the purse while again sewing across the other opening before attaching straps.

FRIENDSHIP AUTOGRAPH SCRAPBOOKS

Just like popular autograph books in decades past, invite teens to write on a page of one another's scrapbooks. Find information on silly rhymes and other things teenagers in the '50s and '60s used to sign in one another's books and show this group. They may decorate each page and have space for more friends to write information.

FRIENDSHIP FRAMES WITH COLLAGES

Teens may decorate their own frames or one to give a friend. Inside the frame can go a collage featuring pictures of friends having fun, accompanied by pictures or decorations from magazines.

BRACELETS

Inspire teens to make older-style friendship bracelets with beads, leather cording, and more. Supply instructions for various designs or go over some with them.

FRIENDSHIP MURAL

All projects should be complete about 15 minutes before the end of the program to allow drying time, though fabric glues will need to dry further at home. During those closing minutes, the girls can enjoy snacks and work on the friendship mural. The mural will be blank butcher paper where girls can take markers and write about why friends are important to them, kind things friends have done for them (with no names), tips on how to be a good friend, or the titles of favorite friendship books or movies.

VARIATIONS

- Many of this program's crafts would work well as shorter stand-alone projects near Valentine's Day or Mother's Day, especially the frames and collages.
- Show a teen friendship movie and do one of the projects.

PROMOTION

- Demonstrate some of the crafts at other local agencies to promote the event.
- Make bookmark flyers that tell teens to bring a friend; tuck them in a display of friendship books.

MARCH MADNESS BASKETBALL AND BOOKS

There is a reason everyone calls March the month of March Madness; tie this program into the hoopla surrounding the NCAA basketball tournament. This program is sure to appeal to sports fans and in particular basketball fans everywhere. You can also add to the fun by tracking the geography of where the competing teams come from and where the games are played. Most of the tournament activity is on the weekends, so plan to have weekly "watch parties" with your teens. Choose one or two games featuring your regional teams and invite teens to watch with snacks or pizza.

PREPARATION TIME

1–2 months for publicity and shopping

LENGTH OF PROGRAM

6 weeks or the duration of the tournament

NUMBER OF TEENS

10–50

SUGGESTED AGE RANGE

Grades 6–12

SHOPPING LIST

☐ Snacks for weekly game watching

☐ Drinks

☐ Prizes (small weekly prizes like treat bags of candy or book giveaways) plus large prizes for tournament winners.

SET IT UP

TWO MONTHS BEFORE

- Begin advertising the program through posters, flyers, and online media outlets. Later, when it's closer to the program and the regional tournaments have started, invite teens to choose their favorite teams and fill out their brackets once the teams are announced.
- Once the final brackets have been announced, make copies to hand out to teens. Add room at the top of the form for library information, the dates of your weekly "watch parties," and teens' name and personal info.
- Before the tournament begins, collect the brackets your teens have filled out and put them in a big decorated box or other container for prize drawings. Draw a big bracket on poster board to put on display.

DAY OF EACH WEEKLY WATCH PARTY

Get the space ready by setting up TVs, comfy seating, and snacks. If serving pizza, order it well in advance because this is a particularly busy time for pizza delivery. Gather three to five small door prizes to give away to teens who attend.

MAKE IT HAPPEN

Whether the library hosts viewing parties or not, keep track of the tournament by recording the winners on a poster-sized display of the entire grid. Enter the names of teens who correctly predict the most game winners into a weekly drawing for small prizes.

VARIATIONS

Instead of having weekly watch parties, host one for the championship game. Or skip the watch parties altogether and just have teens check in weekly to see how well their brackets did. Have drawings for winners or give prizes to teens who come closest to guessing the final score for each game.

PROMOTION

Decorate the teen area with a basketball or sports theme. Booktalk and display basketball or sports-themed books when you visit schools and promote the program. Contact junior high or high school basketball coaches and invite them to participate. For added fun, invite area cheerleaders or dance teams to perform at your watch parties or to kick off or end the program.

TOTALLY TECH LOCK-IN

Teens and technology are a permanent couple. Libraries and technology are another. Put teens together with favorite technologies at an after-hours event. The word *lock-in* can trigger fear on the part of staff, and visions of staying all night with teens in the library, but a lock-in does not have to last overnight. Teens will enjoy being in the library when no one else is, no matter how long. Consider hosting a 4- or 5-hour event with stations and activities that feature the great technologies and services the library has to offer.

Given that YALSA's Teen Tech Week is held each March, that may be a good time to host this event, but it could feature seasonal activities for other times of the year.

PREPARATION TIME

2 months for publicity and shopping

LENGTH OF PROGRAM

5 hours

NUMBER OF TEENS

5–7 per staff member (suggested limit)

SUGGESTED AGE RANGE

Grades 7–10

SHOPPING LIST

- ❑ Gaming platforms, games, and equipment
- ❑ Movies to show
- ❑ Technology craft kits such as CD clocks, magnets to decorate, magnetic frames, paper to make iron-on transfers
- ❑ Ingredients to make microwave nachos, such as chips, cheeses, salsa
- ❑ Snacks such as chips, pop/water, pretzels, popcorn
- ❑ Paper goods such as plates, napkins, bowls, spoons (for sundae bar)
- ❑ Pizza (optional)
- ❑ Ingredients for ice cream sundae bar (optional)
- ❑ Mini prizes for contests or handouts

SET IT UP

TWO MONTHS BEFORE

- Plan activities to fill a 5-hour event. Keep in mind that all teens will not want to watch particular movies, so have at least two things going on most of the time.
- Prepare permission slips or how the drop-offs and pickups will be handled for the evening and publicize that information.
- Organize any additional staff needed.
- Purchase craft kits and any gaming equipment that will be needed.
- Prepare an online scavenger hunt that requires visits to library databases or fun teen Internet sites.

- Purchase food for the evening.
- Contact participating teens to ask about food allergies and go over drop-off and pickup procedures.

DAY OF PROGRAM

- Set up activity stations as much as possible if patrons are still in the building. A half hour before closing, organize staff to sign in participants and get them started on a craft in a meeting room until the library is closed and all have arrived. When teens sign in, ask about any food allergies and remind parents of the pickup procedure. Give parents the number of a cell phone that a staff member will be carrying if the library phones will not be answered after hours.
- Learn how to use the library paging system to make announcements during the evening.

MAKE IT HAPPEN

Go over the rules of the night when the group is all together, as well as the stations and the schedule, if there are planned activities. For example, maybe a Rock Band tournament or a Mario Brawl tournament will be held at a couple of times.

GREAT GAMING

The gaming station should feature a few different platforms and screens for teens. Use the biggest screens available. Teens may play on their own for a while or participate in a couple of announced tournaments. A staff member needs to be present to help with the gaming station.

COMPUTER GAMING

Create a station of computers that teens may use for gaming, Facebook, or other leisure activities. Place the scavenger hunt online for those who may be interested.

MOVIE MADNESS

Dedicate one area for movies and offer popcorn just for that area. Teens can vote on which movies to watch early in the night or show preselected ones.

TECHNO CRAFTS

This station should be available earlier in the evening in case anything needs to dry. Crafts can include CD clocks, magnets to decorate, magnetic frames, or designing iron-on transfers for T-shirts with computer printouts.

MICROWAVE NACHOS

Technology can meet food at a nacho station where teens may make nachos and choose their own toppings.

PIZZA AND SUNDAE BAR

To keep teens fed, it may be a good idea to serve pizza early in the evening and to set up a sundae bar toward the end of the event.

RELAXATION STATION

When teens are not eating, use that area as a Relaxation Station where teens can just hang out, play board games, or read. That way teens can enjoy some downtime while still having other times to participate in activities.

SCAVENGER HUNT

Consider a real scavenger hunt where teens must find things in the library for a team event. Have them find different library equipment to tie in to the technology theme. The sundae bar could be open after that for teams who finish quickly and need something to do.

CART RACING

Cart racing may not be for every library, but could have a technology angle where possible. Put out pieces of old or withdrawn equipment. Teens must add five pieces of equipment to their cart and need to compete to have the fastest cart. This may be done on the sidewalk outside the library, down a hallway, etc.

VARIATIONS

- To create a longer tech-themed festival, present each station's activity as a separate event in a series of weekly programs held in the evening, after school, or on Saturdays.
- Present information on technological things online for a week; for example, the online scavenger hunt one day, instructions on microwave snacks the next, YouTube library movies the third, links to online gaming or tips on doing well in gaming the next.

PROMOTION

- Put posters and flyers in gaming and music stores.
- Promote through all online channels; the nature of this event makes it a natural match for online marketing. Feature links to the games or covers of the games that will be played. Consider putting samples of the crafts in a display case to feature the event or put photos of them online.

8

April

The birds are singing, trees are turning green, and spring is in the air. Fresh air and sunshine bring new teens to the library looking for information to wrap up school projects and creative ways to spend spring break. Spice up a school break with a poetry competition or battle of the books. As the excitement of the glamour and glitz of prom season builds, tap into the interest with a Primp Your Prom program. Help teens reach out to those less fortunate than themselves by hosting a prom dress exchange.

PRIMP YOUR PROM

Spring break is a great time to go all out with programming. Glam up spring break with the Primp Your Prom program. Host a dress exchange to bring new life to last year's prom attire. Maybe invite a makeup artist in to add some fun and color to a glamour style. This is also a good time to talk about prom safety and the perils of drinking and driving by inviting local law enforcement to visit your program for a presentation.

PREPARATION TIME

3–4 months for publicity and gathering donated prom dresses; schedule presenters and a makeup artist, if desired.

LENGTH OF PROGRAM

2 hours

NUMBER OF TEENS

25–50, or more if you are lucky enough to have more donated dresses

SUGGESTED AGE RANGE

Grades 10–12

SHOPPING LIST

- ❑ Snacks such as finger food, cookies, and light-colored punch (so it won't stain the dresses)
- ❑ 4–8 floor-length mirrors—either purchased inexpensively at a discount store or rented from an event planning rental store
- ❑ Sturdy temporary storage racks to hang dresses on
- ❑ Prizes
  - ❑ Gift certificates to hair and nail salons or restaurants
  - ❑ Makeup samples
- ❑ Make Your Own Corsages
  - ❑ Dried flowers and greenery
  - ❑ Floral tape
  - ❑ Glue
  - ❑ Ribbons
  - ❑ Extra large safety pins

SET IT UP

THREE OR FOUR MONTHS BEFORE

Begin advertising the program through posters, flyers, and online media outlets. As part of your publicity campaign, begin soliciting schools, churches, secondhand stores, and others for dress donations. Be sure to request that all donated clothing be dry-cleaned and that all shoes and accessories be cleaned and sanitized. To make this an even more special event, ask for shoes, handbags, men's suits, and ties. Contact salons in the area to ask for gift certificates for free hairstyles, manicures, pedicures, waxes, and tans. Invite the salons to send over staff for makeup and hair demonstrations.

As clothes are donated, double-check their cleanliness and condition. Hang them up and sort them by size, then color and/or style. Don't forget to sort shoes and accessories. Count the available items. You will need to make a numbered drawing slip for each item you are giving away.

TWO HOURS BEFORE

Set up a station for the corsage-making craft. Using wire cutters or strong scissors, trim the stems of the dried flowers and greenery, and separate bunches of flowers into individual blossoms and sprigs. Lay out ribbons, floral tape, glue, and the rest of the supplies. Make a sample corsage to display along with instructions.

MAKE IT HAPPEN

INSTRUCTIONS FOR MAKING CORSAGES

1. Select three or four small buds or flowers and some leaves for greenery.

2. Twist two stems and leaves together with floral tape, then add the other stem and greenery so that the stems are together and the buds or petals are on the outside.

3. Twist the floral tape around again to wind everything together tightly.

4. Wrap colored ribbon around the stems and curl the ends if desired.

As teens enter the program, have them stop at the door and register for door prizes. Also give each teen a number so they will know when it is their turn to choose a dress. Invite teens to munch on snacks and watch makeup demonstrations while they wait for their turn. Avoid a free-for-all with the dresses by calling each teen by number and letting her/him choose three outfits to try on.

VARIATIONS

- Once everyone has chosen an outfit, have a fashion show during which they model their choices for one another. Or kick off the event with a fashion show featuring prom attire borrowed from a local store.
- Invite local law enforcement to talk to teens about alcohol safety and the hazards of drunk driving.
- Invite representatives from the local health department to talk to teens about safe sex, date rape, or other issues.

PROMOTION

Partner with local secondhand stores and display posters. Make posters that feature photos of staff wearing their own prom attire. Contact schools and ask them to share information with students as they purchase their prom tickets.

BATTLE OF THE BOOKS

Book battles are large events that can bring an entire community together in a friendly competition over favorite titles. These events work best when they include more than just your home library, so invite a school in your neighborhood—or several—to join you. Form a committee with a representative from each participating group to help select titles, write questions, make rules, etc.

PREPARATION TIME

6 months

LENGTH OF PROGRAM

Reading times may vary, but plan at least 8 weeks for reading. The battle itself will last about 90 minutes.

NUMBER OF TEENS

100+

SUGGESTED AGE RANGE

Grades 6–12, depending on the books chosen

SHOPPING LIST

- ❑ Pizza, soft drinks, and other snacks
- ❑ Egg timers (one for each group)

SET IT UP

- Create a committee to select a wide variety of books to read for the battle. Choose books with a broad range of reading levels. Look for newer titles that are award winners or nominees, that are popular, and that cover a variety of interest levels. Each committee member should read all of the books selected.

- Create twenty-five trivia questions for each title. Once teens have all been divided into teams, let them choose which books they will read, but encourage them to read as many as possible in order to be better prepared to compete.

MAKE IT HAPPEN

1. On the day of the battle, arrange the room so that each team has its own small space. Provide a timer for each group. Set up a table at the front of the room for three to five judges and a table for snacks at the back of the room. Have the judges take turns asking trivia questions about each book. Either assign each question a point value depending on the question's difficulty or keep track of how many correct answers each team achieves.

2. Once the trivia competition has been completed, compile scores and award prizes or trophies. Either pass out certificates to each participant or spread the awards around by adding fun awards to recognize the achievements of the teens who took part.

VARIATIONS

Have genre-specific battles: all mysteries or fantasies, etc. Have an all-out challenge described above or have rounds of challenges, beginning with individual classes challenging each other to determine a school winner, who then challenges another school's winner to arrive at a citywide winner.

PROMOTION

Promote through competing schools, groups, etc. Challenge school officials and civic leaders to become involved. Create bookmarks with book battle titles to hand out to teens.

POETRY SLAM

Poetry slams are wonderful competitive events for serious poetry lovers. Slammers typically read only poems that they have written themselves. Open rounds can start the competition or involve anyone who would like to join in and read their creations.

PREPARATION TIME

1–2 months

LENGTH OF PROGRAM

90 minutes

NUMBER OF TEENS

20–50

SUGGESTED AGE RANGE

Grades 9–12

SHOPPING LIST
- ❑ Coffees
- ❑ Teas
- ❑ Baked goods
- ❑ Cream and sugar
- ❑ Cups, napkins, plates, spoons

SET IT UP

Solicit judges to help choose winners. Talk to local English teachers, poets, authors, and staff members. Set up a stage area where poets will read and a space where the audience can comfortably enjoy the poetry slam. Set up a judges' area near the stage so that the judges have a good view of the audience and the stage where the poets are performing. Set out snacks and beverages.

MAKE IT HAPPEN

In round 1, each teen who wishes to participate will have a chance to read their poetry. Decide on a time limit for reading and appoint a timekeeper who sits at the judges' table but is not a judge. If there are rules about language usage or anything else, remind teens before they begin. Invite the audience to cheer and applaud after each performance to indicate their level of appreciation. Have the judges assign each reading a score of 1 to 10 based on audience feedback. At the end of the round, tally the points and announce the readers with the highest scores, who will then move on to the next round. Repeat until a winner is declared.

VARIATIONS

Create a team of poetry readers to represent the library at other slams. Prepare the team by asking a local teacher or poet to present some poetry-writing workshops. To help teens become acclimated to reading in front of an audience, set up a poetry café where they can practice in a noncompetitive environment.

PROMOTION

Collaborate with area schools. Write a rhyming ad or limerick to read over the PA system or on the radio. Create booklists and bookmarks with names of poetry books and how-to books on writing poetry.

9

May

May is a really busy month for teens, especially older ones. They are finishing the end of the school year with plays, concerts, awards celebrations, and social activities. But some teens may still be looking for more to do or for some way to take a creative break from end-of-the-year stress. The Magic Moment Writing Challenge may be just the thing.

Teens may also be looking for summer jobs, if they have not lined something up already. Competition is stronger than ever for such positions, with many unemployed adults willing to take any job to bring in money. That makes May a fitting time to host a job skills program to coach teens on etiquette for interviews and applications.

It is also time to gear up for summer reading. Kickoff events do not have to be expensive and elaborate to set the mood for a great summer at the public library.

MAGIC MOMENT WRITING CHALLENGE

Ask teens to write about a moment in time, a life-changing, memorable moment. Likely we all remember our first kiss, or winning an award, or sad moments. A short writing contest with a fun prize may well inspire even teens who do not think they can write to enter. Teachers looking for a fun final assignment may want to enter entire classes as well!

PREPARATION TIME

6 weeks to promote the contest

LENGTH OF PROGRAM

1 month for the contest to run

NUMBER OF TEENS

No limit

SUGGESTED AGE RANGE

Grades 7–12

SHOPPING LIST

- ❑ Gift certificates to an area bookstore for prizes
- ❑ Digital video camera to make Magic Moment movies (optional)
- ❑ Books to reward teachers who enter entire classrooms in the contest (optional)

SET IT UP

SIX WEEKS BEFORE

- Begin developing and marketing the contest right after spring break to build momentum.
- Define guidelines for the contest. Will the contest be based on an actual moment teens have experienced or can they create a fictional one? Teens may not feel they have had magical moments, and the fictional option may welcome more entries.
- Will separate winners be chosen from junior and senior high? If you usually get a lot of teacher support and entries into contests, this is a good option. Can teens enter more than once? If so, make it clear that teens cannot win more than one prize, as you may have a talented teen who sweeps the event, discouraging others.
- Decide who will judge the contest. Usually a combination of teens and adults works well. It is possible to have staff narrow it down to five to ten finalists, then community members or teens rank the winners.
- The number of winners should not be advertised ahead of time if this is the first or second time hosting this contest, in case a large or very small number of teens enter. If this contest has run a few times and staff can comfortably estimate the number of entries, it is safer to advertise what the top three or five winners will receive. This gives staff flexibility with prizes, too.
- If the contest is running the entire month of May, decide when winning names will be posted and in what form. If there is a lot of interest, teens will be looking for this information, and with the

end of the school year arriving in early June, staff may want to post the winners within a few days of the end of the contest. Consider offering it for half the month as another alternative. Teen interest may wane by the end of the month, and judges may welcome the extra time.

MAKE IT HAPPEN

1. During the first day that teens can turn in scenes, send out electronic reminders about the event. They should already know about it from your advance marketing and displays in the library.

2. When an entry arrives by e-mail or other electronic means, send a confirmation to the writer and record it in a list of entrants' names and dates of submission. It is helpful to include contact information in this database so you can notify all participants about the winners and promote upcoming library events. If a teacher turns in an entire packet of entries, track each writer individually. Consider thanking teachers who participate by sending them a token gift, such as a book.

3. Send out another reminder about halfway through the event to keep it fresh in teen minds. At the beginning of the contest, many teens who really want to enter will see they have a lot of time and put it off. (Like adults!)

4. Prepare a letter to teens who will not win to send out quickly, either through e-mail or by snail mail, after results are made public. The letter should encourage them to continue writing and suggest writing resources available at the library, upcoming writing and author events, and ways teens can get published. Notifying only the winners and ignoring the other entrants can be discouraging. Some may be new at putting themselves on the line and may attach more importance to what staff might see as a simple writing contest than previously thought. A well-worded letter thanking teens for their effort, even if it was not a strong entry, can create lifelong library fans.

5. Begin judging immediately after the contest closes. As finalists are chosen, promptly send out the letters to those who did not win. When the winners are chosen, send any remaining letters to non-winners and post the winners along with winning themes.

6. It is possible you'll get contest entries with mature or delicate subject matter. Consider posting the teen's first name and grade with the winning scenes rather than complete information for all. They will still see their work published, but this offers some insulation against reaction; for example, if a teen writes a scene about telling her mother she is a lesbian. Or another teen writes a well-crafted scene with sexual content.

VARIATIONS

- It is easy enough to hold a Themed Magic Moment Contest: holiday gift, first day of school, dance, sports or music performance, summer or winter, friendship moments, and more can adapt this program for any time of the year. If the first Magic Moment Contest is popular, offering another with a theme within the same year may retain interest.
- Consider setting limits to build interest if there are usually small numbers of teens participating at the library. For example, the first twenty-five to enter could win a fine-clearing coupon or another coupon toward extra DVD or game checkouts.
- During nights or afternoons with lots of teens present, hand out the worksheets and let teens know it is Mad Magic Moment time in the library, letting them know you will be available to collect entries when they finish. While no doubt some will laugh, some may stop everything and write.
- If staff and teens made Magic Moment Movies to promote the contest or as a reward for winning entries (see description under "Promotion"), consider offering a Magic Moment Night where scenes would be acted out live or shown from short movie clips of the teens' entries.

- Use one or several photos for teens to describe a magic moment. This is a good writing exercise and activity for a writing club as well.

PROMOTION

- Contact local schools through electronic updates or with worksheets about the contest. The worksheets could have space for teens to handwrite their entries. Also begin sending electronic reminders to teens about the event. It is possible that they will receive the e-mail, Tweet, Facebook notice, or whatever electronic bulletin and write in right away. Post resources or actual examples of memorable moments from movies and books to further inspire.
- For a more elaborate promotion, you could set up Magic Moment Commercials in YouTube with teens in library clubs who would act out moments. Or perhaps the first five to ten students to enter the contest could help develop their scene into a Magic Moment Movie. They could either act it out with friends or participate with Teen Advisory Board members.
- Highlight the event on a bulletin board in an area where students will be doing lots of end-of-year studying. With *magic* in the title of this contest, displays can easily be eye-catching, with star scenes, descriptive photos of important moments, or other tie-ins to the magic or time themes. Be sure to have lots of copies of the worksheet nearby. It should be clear and easy for teens to turn in worksheets or send in electronic scenes for this event.

JOB SKILLS FOR SUCCESSFUL TEENS

While proactive teens may be lining up jobs for the summer during their spring break, some teens will still be looking for work in June. With the recent economic problems, fewer jobs are available for teens as out-of-work adults compete with them for the same positions in retail outlets. Keep information on organizations that use teen volunteers or any that hire teens regularly for the summer, such as park district pools. A job skills workshop is never a bad idea, though, as teens will be able to use these techniques for years to come.

PREPARATION TIME

3 months for publicity, from spring break on

LENGTH OF PROGRAM

90 minutes

NUMBER OF TEENS

50 maximum

SUGGESTED AGE RANGE

Grades 9–12

SHOPPING LIST

- ❑ Samples of inappropriate and appropriate clothes for interviews
- ❑ Applications from several local places that hire teens in multiple copies for teens to practice (a laptop at the program with online applications open would also work)
- ❑ Samples of bad applications turned in to the library from at least a few years back, or make up inappropriate answers
- ❑ Snacks for the program
- ❑ Sample of folder teens may want to bring to interview

SET IT UP

TWO MONTHS BEFORE

- Contact local retail outlets, agencies, or library staff who hire teens to see if someone could come speak to teens about interviewing and applications.
- Invite teens who work at the library to come for a part of the program to talk about their experience including dress, demeanor, and work ethic.
- Talk with work/study instructors at local schools to see if they or their students would be available to discuss briefly their experiences and favorite aspects of their work.
- Make a list of local places that could possibly be hiring teens for the summer. Also add places that would utilize teen volunteers.
- Ask local agencies to help advertise the program with flyers and posters. Put information about the program near the employment link on the library website if one is available.

DAY OF PROGRAM

Pull resources on résumé writing and interviewing. Set out snacks. Arrange chairs around tables so teens can write and set out sample applications, scratch paper, and pencils and pens.

MAKE IT HAPPEN

1. As teens enter the room, invite them to begin listing their skills on scratch paper, including classes they excel in, languages they speak, clubs, interests, projects, volunteer work, and computer experience.

2. Once most teens have arrived, begin with the guest speakers so they may leave after their discussion. Allow each speaker at least 10 minutes to discuss their role—either as a teen worker, an instructor, or someone who hires teens—and a few minutes for questions. (Consider thanking speakers for their time by giving them something like a signed book.)

3. Invite teens to list jobs their friends have or where they have seen teens working. List those jobs on a board, and then list some job skills each experience gives teens for the future. Even a fast-food job provides multitasking and customer service skills. Explain that even if you want to be a doctor and a fast-food job seems irrelevant, customer service skills always come in handy. Briefly talk about networking: the same teen who works fast food and wants to be a doctor is kind to someone who works in a hospital who may help them get an entry-level position there.

4. Discuss how to fill out applications. Give examples of phrases that are not illustrative of skills, like "knows computers," and how that could be rewritten. Go over an entire application with the group, inviting responses.

5. Discuss how to ask for an application and how to turn one in. Explain that parents should not be doing this for teens who want a job and that demeanor even when asking a clerk for an application makes an impression on staff.

6. Go over interview techniques. Invite teens to list what interviewees should not do, and invite some to give bad examples of interviews with skits. Then give an example of a good interview with a teen volunteer.

7. Explain what happens once teens are hired, from filling out tax forms to training, to procedures for appropriately taking days off. Discuss confidentiality and responsibility and ask for examples where that would be needed.

SKITS AND SCENARIOS

Give teen groups a scenario to act out or discuss

- what to do if a coworker is stealing supplies
- what to do if there are inappropriate adult behaviors directed at working teens
- what to do if a supervisor asks a teen to close by themselves each night and it is not safe
- what are appropriate reasons for and ways to quit a job
- what are some techniques for handling nasty customers
- how to handle constructive criticism on the job

VARIATIONS

- This program could be run by representatives from the local chamber of commerce or other business representatives.
- Ask a local agency to draw for an automatic interview for a teen at the program.
- Discuss ways teens could start their own business based on their skills with SCORE representatives or local businesspeople.

PROMOTION

- Set up outfits on mannequins or pin them to a bulletin board, with one inappropriate outfit for an interview and one appropriate, and invite teens to vote on which is better.
- Put posters and flyers up at local agencies and retail outlets that hire teens that begin by asking teens if they are looking for ways to earn spending money.

SUMMER READING KICKOFF

This program is different from other listings in this book as it will provide several different ways to begin summer reading events. For a school library, these could be applied to a reading initiative or special festival week at the school or to a yearlong reading program.

PREPARATION TIME

1 month for publicity

LENGTH OF PROGRAM

Either 2 hours for a big event or 1 week for other options listed below

NUMBER OF TEENS

No limit needed for most options

SUGGESTED AGE RANGE

Grades 7–12

SHOPPING LIST

❑ Most options described below include prize handouts for summer reading sign-ups.

SET IT UP

ONE MONTH BEFORE

- Summer reading may require less publicity than other events, as many people already expect to find it at the library. Garner attention by sending coupons out to middle and junior high schools who may be experiencing teen summer reading for the first time, inviting teens to turn in the coupons for a prize when registering for summer reading.
- If hosting a big event to kick off the summer reading program, hire and confirm performers well in advance.
- The teen collection areas should be decorated in some way to reflect the upcoming exciting summer events. Invite teen groups to do this.

MAKE IT HAPPEN

- Many libraries host a big kickoff celebration for teens for summer reading, such as a band night, bike acrobat groups, or other events that are popular but usually cannot be held at other times of the year. To tie these in to the program, consider handing out tickets to the event when teens register for summer reading.
- While kickoff events definitely garner attention and publicity, they are hard to schedule. Summer school sessions often begin the week after finals or when school lets out. Many families go on vacation during this time. Other variations to celebrate summer reading and motivate teens to register for it are listed below.

- Themed events will continue to draw attention to the program. If the summer reading theme is mysteries, schedule mystery programs early in the summer, such as the two outlined in the July chapter in this book. Themed displays should be prominent for teens.

- Celebrate the beginning of summer reading for an entire week to capture teens' attention. This could be done with a table staffed in the lobby with teen volunteers, ready to register their fellow teens for the program. Hold a drawing each day for teens who have registered so that those who signed up early get more chances.
- Offer simple prizes to those who sign up during the first week or to the first hundred teens who sign up. Offer prizes to teens when their entire family registers for summer reading at the library.
- If the summer reading program requires teens to turn in book review forms to qualify for prizes, consider offering twice the value of tickets for those turned in during the first month of the program or a big drawing at the end of the first month to encourage participation.

VARIATIONS

- Reading kickoff events could be held to celebrate a winter reading program with an after-hours indoor event when weather is bad.
- A weeklong festival would work for National Library Week, Teen Read Week, or Teen Tech Week, with themed tie-ins as well.
- Initiatives for teens who register for library cards could have similar promotions, from tickets for prizes to drawings for the first one hundred teens who clear their cards or register for new ones during September for National Library Card Month.

PROMOTION

- Provide coupons for middle schools and junior highs to exchange for a prize when registering for summer reading. Coupons could also be put in brochures and newsletters or sent online to older teens as well.
- Register teens at all clubs and programs for summer reading during the entire first month of summer.
- Invite local agencies such as pools that may desire teen summer business to cross-promote with coupons or prizes.
- Have a teen volunteer decorating event for the reading program, where teens could design and put up themed items. During the first week of the program, balloons or cutouts hanging from the ceiling could be added to draw more attention.

June

Summer events for public libraries get into high gear when school lets out. More teens will be coming in, and perhaps new teens and families will be coming in for the first time to get required summer reading items for local schools or items for vacations. Some parents will be bringing in teens to find out how to fill their time in the summer.

It is fun to host more elaborate programs in the summer, when many teens have more time to participate. Consider hosting a teen program on a particular night each week, with a few on other dates and times, so teens know to come each week for certain activities at that time. A few ideas for programs for summer are provided here. Techno Book Discussions will feature different ways to host book programs with interactive games or using technology. Mystery Madness is a dinner event requiring one rehearsal with teen volunteer cast members ahead of time, so June may provide an opportunity to take part in that. Get a Clue in the Library continues the mystery scene while allowing teens to write about crime scenes.

TECHNO BOOK DISCUSSIONS

Technology and teens go together, and it is time to take book discussions in a new direction by bringing in some creativity and technology. Teens will love sharing their opinions and talking about their favorite books when you use technology to spread the discussion.

PREPARATION TIME

1 month

LENGTH OF PROGRAM

60 minutes

NUMBER OF TEENS

20–30

SUGGESTED AGE RANGE

Grades 6–12

SHOPPING LIST

- ❑ Snacks
- ❑ Beverages
- ❑ Serving utensils
- ❑ Paper products
- ❑ Prizes

SET IT UP

Choose a title that your teens will enjoy reading and talking about. A title published in paperback is a good choice because it is less expensive and easier to purchase in bulk. If teens are responsible for providing their own copy of the book, consider purchasing additional copies for the collection and use the opportunity to introduce teens to the interlibrary loan process in their search for copies to read. Read the book and create a list of topics to explore.

MAKE IT HAPPEN

1. PowerPoint versions of popular TV games are popular ways to easily bring technology into the mix. There are tons of easily obtainable instructions for creating a PowerPoint version of *Jeopardy*, *Are You Smarter Than a Fifth Grader*, *Family Feud*, and more.

2. Book trailers are another tech activity that teens will enjoy. They can be a discussion tool if you have teens find pictures online that represent favorite scenes in the book your group is discussion. Put each teen's image on a PowerPoint slide and either type out or record the description of the image and its relation to the book. Order the slides according to when they occur in the story. When you show the slides, pause and let the teens discuss each one.

VARIATIONS

When you are thinking about technology and teens, don't forget about the impact of social and viral tools to add some fun. Open up discussions on some of the social networking sites that are popular with your teens.

PROMOTION

Advertise your program on your library website. Send teens reminders or calendar notes by e-mail or text message. Use social networking tools to help spread the word.

MYSTERY MADNESS

In *A Year of Programs for Teens*, author Amy Alessio provided a sample mystery dinner outline with character sketches. In response to reader requests, here is another mystery program that will be easy for staff to run with help from teen volunteers.

This style of mystery dinner requires at least one run-through with teens ahead of time, but not elaborate hours of rehearsal. The script revolves around a pizza restaurant and works well when the audience is served pizza while the mystery goes on.

PREPARATION TIME

1 month, including rehearsal time

LENGTH OF PROGRAM

90 minutes

NUMBER OF TEENS

50, plus 8–11 teen cast members

SUGGESTED AGE RANGE

Grades 7–12

SHOPPING LIST

- ❑ Pizza for cast and audience
- ❑ Drinks
- ❑ Ice cream sundae bar supplies
    - ❑ Ice cream
    - ❑ Sprinkles
    - ❑ Whipped cream
    - ❑ Toppings
    - ❑ Nuts

- ❑ Cherries
- ❑ Bananas
- ❑ Oreos or crushed cookies
- ❑ Wafers
- ❑ Gummy worms
- ❑ Paper goods for serving
- ❑ Props for mystery
  - ❑ Baggies
  - ❑ Gloves
  - ❑ Camera
  - ❑ Tweezers for CSI techs
  - ❑ Sign for door: "Pizza Pete's Restaurant"
  - ❑ Partially used bottle of spray cleaning solution
- ❑ Each character should dress their part with any props they feel they need; for example, the detective could have a badge, a notebook, and a pen
- ❑ Prizes for the winning team and for most creative team, possibly mystery books or detective kits, or gift certificates for pizza

SET IT UP

ONE MONTH BEFORE

- Recruit teen volunteers and match them to parts. Most parts can be played by either a male or a female. Send cast members just their profile and the questions they will be asked, along with the time line for the evening.
- Make a handout for the audience that includes a brief description of each character, along with space for notes. See the section below on "Interrogation Information for the Cast" for more information about what audience members should know versus what cast members know. Create forms for teens to turn in—one per table—of who was the murderer and why.

TWO WEEKS BEFORE

Go over the entire evening with the cast. Some may need to review their interrogation a few times. This should not take more than 90 minutes.

DAY OF PROGRAM

Set up the room and order the pizzas.

THIRTY MINUTES BEFORE

The cast should be in place a half hour before the program begins.

MAKE IT HAPPEN

CHARACTERS

- Pizza Pete Pastachio
- Paul Pastachio
- Phil Pastachio
- Kurt Hartake
- Edwina Moolah

- Louise Luvacuccio
- Margot Glamore
- Olive Sparkle
- Detective Temper
- CSI techs (up to three)

PROPS

- ❑ Sign for door indicating that the room is Pizza Pete's Restaurant
- ❑ Room set up like a restaurant with tables and chairs
- ❑ Table at the front of the room for interrogations

SETUP

- Kurt Hartake greets audience members as they come in and helps seat them. He will then serve pizza from the kitchen to the three brothers and Louise, who will be sitting at the front of the room.
- Olive will be clearing up in the kitchen, where people can see her.
- Edwina will be walking around muttering angrily.
- Margot will be walking around furtively.
- Guests should come in and enjoy the pizza and beverages. On their tables are pencils, the overviews of the cast members, including Pizza Pete (as he will not yet be dead), and forms to fill out about who killed the victim and why.

ACTION

(When most of audience has arrived)

- Pizza Pete is enjoying a nice dinner with friends when suddenly he screams, clutches at his throat, and falls to the floor.
- Staff will call 9-1-1, and the police and the crime scene techs will take over. They will discuss the body, take fingerprints with the CSI kit, pick up things with tweezers, use chemicals, and throw a sheet over the body. They will also take pictures. They will pick up the pepperoni and put it into baggies. The techs leave but quickly come back to talk with the detective loud enough for everyone to hear. They are concerned because they could not find the container from the cleaning solvent that probably killed Pete, though they suspect that some of the liquid was dumped on a plant that is dying at the front of the restaurant. They found shards of plastic in the now-jammed incinerator.
- At intermission, Pizza Pete will be carried out or will subtly sneak out of the room.
- The Detective announces that there has been a murder and that no one is to leave. He will then interrogate suspects. He will call up each suspect and ask them questions based on their profiles. Then the characters will circulate among the tables while the guests ask them questions.
- The guests will be invited up to dessert, then have a few minutes to decide who the killer is before turning in their sheets. The first team to turn in their sheet with the correct answers wins.

INTERROGATION INFORMATION FOR THE CAST

The following information should be given to all the cast ahead of time for rehearsals. It contains everything they need for their characters as well as the questions to be asked by the Detective during the show.

The audience may be given a sheet with a list of characters and brief descriptions—enough to introduce each person and keep them straight but not enough to give away the plot.

PIZZA PETE PASTACHIO is a famous pizza chef with a restaurant in Schaumburg, Illinois. *Although there is no interrogation of the dead man, this information can be used by all the rest of the suspects.* He has a best-selling cookbook and claims the recipes come from Venice, Italy, where his two brothers run a famous restaurant. He has a heavy gambling habit and planned on taking his money and going to the Bahamas soon where he could become a professional gambler.

LOUISE LUVACUCCIO, a former computer tech in a big corporation, wanted to become a chef and worked long shifts as a waitress in Pete's restaurant. They dated for three years, but Pete never talked about marriage. She developed many of the award-winning recipes but is painfully shy and was happy to let Pete take the credit—until recently. She spent many afternoons weeping on Kurt's shoulder. She found out about Pete's girlfriend this morning when she heard the argument with Edwina and knew the money was going to the girlfriend. She saw a bottle of cleaning fluid, sprayed it on the pepperoni slices before serving it. Then she had second thoughts and decided to eat it herself and die dramatically in front of Pete. She switched the plates just before they were served in the kitchen, setting it up so she would receive the poisoned pepperoni. She stopped in the powder room to get her nerve up and wipe away her tears, then went out to join the brothers for dinner.

Name _____

Occupation? You also did some cooking? _____

Relationship with Pete _____

I've heard you were his fiancée. How did you feel about that? _____

What time did you come in? _____

What did you do when you came in? Did you do any cleaning? Was there anyone else in the kitchen?

_____

You ate with Pete and his two brothers? What time? _____

What did you talk about? _____

Who served the pizza? _____

You didn't put anything in the pizza, did you? _____

You overheard the argument between Pete and Edwina Moolah, didn't you? _____

What were they arguing about? _____

I understand that Pete was seeing Margot Glamore? _____

Were you aware of Kurt's interest in you? _____

Did you use the cleaning solution? Did you put it in the pizza? _____

PHIL PASTACHIO and **PAUL PASTACHIO** are Pete's brothers from Italy. They speak limited English and will converse in (phony) Italian or broken phrases before responding to each question from the Detective. They especially cannot understand any questions about where their family money comes from. In fact, their restaurant is not doing well since their mother became ill and no longer cooks for them. Their mother was an infamous assassin in Italy as well. They came here hoping to steal Pete's new recipes and use them in the family restaurant in Italy.

Name _____

Relationship with Pete _____

What was your role in Pete's restaurant? _____

What were you discussing with Pete when he died? _____

What was the last thing Pete said to you? _____

What time did you arrive? _____

Why are you here in the United States? _____

Mother's restaurant? Why didn't your mother come with you? Word is that your mother is a hit man for the Mafia. She doesn't put things in the pizza that don't belong there, does she?

_____

How did you feel about Pete's death? _____

EDWINA MOOLAH is the banker who gave the money to Pasta Pete for his restaurant. She knew the Pastachios in Italy and gave Pete the money after she tasted Louise's pizza. Pete recently asked for more money to "expand his business." Edwina gave him an undocumented loan and kept the interest herself. Pete recently found this out when he visited the bank to make an extra payment and had an argument with Edwina before tonight's dinner.

Name _____

Occupation? _____

Relationship with Pete _____

What time did you arrive? What did you do between the time you arrived and when Pete died?

_____

Why were you here tonight? _____

Had an argument with Pete? _____

Checking financial records found some irregularities. High interest? The bank charges that high of an interest? Loaned him your money, not the bank's? _____

KURT HARTAKE is the host at the restaurant and a medical student. Kurt is the killer, and this character needs to be cagey while avoiding discussing the following information: He is in love with Louise and switched the pizza slices after watching her spray the slice and serve it to herself. He thought she made a mistake serving it to herself and made sure that Pete ate it instead. Then he dumped the cleaning solution in a plant behind the restaurant and put the bottle in the incinerator, after wiping it down. Kurt saw Louise in the kitchen when he came in from his smoking break, then came in to switch the plates. Then he went to his post at the door.

Name _____

Occupation? Medical student? _____

What was your relationship with Pete? _____

What time did you arrive? _____

What did you do after you arrived? Did you see anybody else in the kitchen? _____

You served the pizza? Did you serve individual slices? Was there anybody in the kitchen when you left? _____

What was your relationship with Louise Luvacuccio? You seem more interested in Louise than just as a coworker. _____

Who usually does the cleaning in the kitchen? _____

Did you know about Pete's other girlfriend? _____

Did their relationship bother you? _____

MARGOT GLAMORE is the Internet girlfriend who has been dating Pete online through the library computers. Pete is not her only boyfriend—in fact, she solicits men from all over and they give her money, plane tickets, anything—then she disappears. She met Pete in person a month ago and told him she needed money to leave her current boyfriend. He gave her a plane ticket to the Bahamas. She really liked Pete and was coming to the restaurant tonight to reimburse him for the ticket.

Name _____

Occupation? Unemployed? _____

Relationship with Pete? How long? _____

Did you have other relationships with men you met on the Internet? They gave you gifts, money?

_____

Did you know that Pete was already seeing Louise Luvacuccio? _____

How did you feel about that?_____

Why did you come to visit Pete at this time? _____

What did Pete give you money for? _____

Checking financial records found two one-way tickets to the Bahamas . . . _____

OLIVE SPARKLE is the head of the cleaning staff for the restaurant. She takes her job very, very seriously. She was upset when she couldn't find her cleaning solution tonight as she noticed a thumbprint on the door. She went to find the solution around 6:10. She had not seen it since 5:30, when she was cleaning the mirrors in the washroom. Her Italian grandmother was killed by the brothers' mother, and she had not yet figured out what she wanted to do for revenge.

Name _____

Occupation? _____

What was your relationship with Pete? Good boss? _____

What time did you arrive? _____

What did you do after you arrived? Cleaning solution? Mirrors? _____

Where were you when Pete died? _____

Grandmother? Trouble between your family and the Pistachios? _____

AFTER THE INTERROGATION

- Consider offering a sundae bar after the interrogation while inviting cast members to circulate once more. The audience should have all the information they need from the interrogation; this is not necessary, but heightens the drama and lengthens the time. Staff should mark the time each form is turned in from audience members with the name of the killer and the reason.
- After the forms have been turned in, have Detective Temper go over the incorrect guesses, first asking the wrong cast members if they did it. They will deny it. When the Detective gets to Kurt, Kurt should proclaim that he did it to save Louise, be arrested by the Detective, and led out. Close the program by awarding prizes to the winning team and the team that came up with the most creative response.

VARIATIONS

This program may be presented without serving pizza to the audience. It could also be done as a fund-raiser while charging money at the door or with and for adult audiences. At the Schaumburg Township District Library it was done as a staff program by staff for staff, with registration fees going to charity.

PROMOTION

- Do not make posters indicating murder in the library. Rather, invite teens to an evening at Pizza Pete's where they may be needed to solve a crime among a cast of suspects.
- Put up a display of the "Mystery Madness" booklist titles from chapter 3 with cutout footprints leading teens from another department up to it, where program information would also be featured.
- Make sample badges with program information on them to hand out at events the month before the program. This badge will indicate that teens are deputized to come help solve the case.

GET A CLUE IN THE LIBRARY

This program features some forensics techniques on "crime scenes" in the library. It would also be a good activity for a creative writing club as they imagine scenes and clues. For this event, crime scenes need to be set up throughout the library, so it may work best as an after-hours event if possible. It is still workable during business hours, but each scene would be set up before teens find it.

PREPARATION TIME

4 hours

LENGTH OF PROGRAM

1 hour; 90 minutes if an expert speaker is presenting also

NUMBER OF TEENS

25

SUGGESTED AGE RANGE

Grades 6–10

SHOPPING LIST

- ☐ Fingerprint powder and brushes
- ☐ Scotch tape (book tape works even better)
- ☐ Magnifying glasses
- ☐ Graph paper and pencils
- ☐ Props for crime scenes—items strewn to show evidence of crimes (suggestions below)
- ☐ Prizes for best detectives: possibly a mystery book or a detective kit

SET IT UP

TWO MONTHS BEFORE

- Contact the local police department to see if anyone is available to discuss evidence collection with the teens. Another idea is to contact the nearest mystery writers groups to see if there is a police mystery author available to help run the program. This was done in a different form by mystery authors Michael A. Black and Dave Case, Chicago-area policemen. Those gentlemen run programs for adults and teens with one large crime scene. They do an elaborate crime scene with evidence reports, mannequin victims, and more. They can be contacted through their websites, www.michaelablack.com or www.davecasebooks.com.
- It is great to have actual professionals do the program to help debunk CSI techniques teens may have seen on TV. Mystery authors often do this type of program for adults as well. It is possible to run this program with just library staff, if fingerprint powder and even crime scene tape can be obtained from local police or online.
- To make a library display of a mini crime scene with information about the program to get attention, section off a small area and put a cup with lipstick, papers, spilled books, etc., and a poster of the event inviting teens to come solve "crimes."
- Line up a few staff helpers to act as witnesses.

- Gather props for each crime scene if this will be done throughout the library.
- Prepare handouts for participants to fill out, asking what happened at the library and how they figured it out.

DAY OF PROGRAM

Set up the three crime scenes for teens to solve and make certain they are sectioned off if the library is still open and patrons will be around those areas. Get "witnesses" in position before the program begins, with one at each station.

MAKE IT HAPPEN

As teens come in, give them pencils, graph paper, and a handout and tell them a crime has been committed in the library and that a teen volunteer is now missing. Outline how fingerprint powder works and how to lift fingerprints. If an expert speaker is participating, they can discuss realistic evidence collection techniques before teens are released to solve the scenes. Give them at least 10 minutes at each scene before they need to return to the room to fill out their reports.

Scene 1. Set up outside the doors of the library. The "janitor" discovered a mess outside the library after closing time. Teens may ask him questions, but he just found it all a few minutes before closing. He had been by 15 minutes prior to check the doors and had seen nothing.

- The scene has a shoe on the ground, crumpled papers, a cell phone, a school jersey or indication of a team sport player for the local high school, and a streak of blood (paint) on wall of library, as if someone hit it.
- A teen or two may check the cell phone for fingerprints. (Fingerprint dust is best used at the outdoor scene.)

Scene 2. Set up in the area near the teen seating in the library. A "librarian" overheard a boy and a girl talking loudly and asked them to be quiet two times. She thought she saw the boy grab the girl's wrist, but when she went back a third time to ask them to leave, they saw her coming and the boy fled. The girl apologized but packed up quickly and followed him, leaving some things behind. That was 15 minutes before closing.

- Items: Photo or torn page from yearbook. College acceptance letter torn in half. Two cups, one with lipstick, strewn across table. Female watch. Overturned chair.

Scene 3. College resource center or area where those materials are kept. No witnesses but the "reference librarian" who found the mess half an hour before closing. Books need to be pulled off and papers strewn on the floor. A necklace with a heart will be on the floor.

- Once teens have investigated all three crime scenes, they should return to the room and work with their teams to describe what happened at each scene and why they think that. The team that comes closest to what likely happened (staff can decide ahead of time what happened in what order) wins. Another prize could be given to most imaginative answer, or a name could be drawn from the entire group for a prize.
- It is a good idea to go over some teen crime subtlety ahead of time, such as the prevalence of teens sending nude photos of themselves and what laws that could break or dating violence. Those are good information, plus they color the story the teens will discover.

VARIATIONS

Set up a scene as a display and invite teens to turn in sheets describing what they think happened during Teen Read Week or other celebrations.

PROMOTION

Make flyers indicating that a crime has been committed in the library and volunteers are needed to solve it, or "Like *CSI*? Put your detective skills to the test" on posters.

July

In July public libraries are in the height of summer events. July is a good time to plan both elaborate and simpler events to capture both older and younger teens. It is also a good time to get the attention of teens who have come in only to get a required summer reading title for a local school or a teen who does not normally have time to stop by during the school year.

A BBQ Books program combines two things many teens like: food and books for a more elaborate event. A Songwriting Contest puts a spin on the traditional poetry contest and is a venue for music lovers. And an Art Media Mixer allows staff to find out the kinds of art local teens like and are good at by letting them try samples of a variety of media in one creative afternoon.

BBQ BOOKS

Summer cookouts and libraries may not be a usual combination, but a Friday evening cookout can be a great way to kick off summer reading, wrap it all up, or just kind of mark the halfway point of the summer break. Food, games, music, and books will turn this activity into a summer tradition.

PREPARATION TIME

1 month

LENGTH OF PROGRAM

2 hours

NUMBER OF TEENS

25+

SUGGESTED AGE RANGE

Grades 6–12

SHOPPING LIST

- ❑ Menu items, including:
    - ❑ Hot dogs or sandwiches
    - ❑ Condiments
    - ❑ Buns
    - ❑ Salads
    - ❑ Desserts
    - ❑ Sodas or beverages
    - ❑ Ice
- ❑ Paper products
- ❑ Door prizes

SET IT UP

If adequate outside space is available, set up tables, chairs, and stations for food and entertainment outside. If not, host the event inside and use decorations to help present an outside atmosphere. Pre-grill hot dogs and keep them warm in crock pots or warmers. Set out food and beverages. Hook up an iPod or other stereo component to speakers for fun background music. Set out some board games, crafts, or other activities for teens to enjoy while they socialize.

MAKE IT HAPPEN

Welcome teens and have them fill out registration slips for door prizes. Allow teens to mingle and wander freely. Provide the food and the fun atmosphere and let the rest take care of itself. Don't forget to give out door prizes near the end of the program.

VARIATIONS

Organize outdoor games and relays for more competitive fun. Invite local teen bands to provide musical entertainment.

PROMOTION

Spread the word about this event when you promote summer reading.

SONGWRITING CONTEST

Although many schools and libraries offer Battle of the Bands programs, smaller facilities may not have a venue for that type of program. Sponsoring a songwriting contest allows smaller places to offer something for young musicians without having to set up a concert.

PREPARATION TIME

2 hours for publicity and shopping

LENGTH OF PROGRAM

1 month

NUMBER OF TEENS

No limit

SUGGESTED AGE RANGE

Grades 9–12

SHOPPING LIST

❑ Prizes for winners, such as gift certificates to music stores or blank journals

SET IT UP

TWO MONTHS BEFORE

- Select judges and categories for contest. Also, determine how tunes will be submitted, whether or not they will be on MP3 files or CDs, downloaded to a particular site, or e-mailed to the library.
- Begin promotion. Consider featuring song lyrics from popular artists in displays or holding a mini contest in which teens would match the lyrics to the song/artist.

MAKE IT HAPPEN

As entries come in, consider saving them all to one CD or file while also keeping track of them in a database. Be sure to open and listen to each entry as it arrives, as some may present technical difficulties and staff will need to let teens know so they have a chance to fix it and reenter.

Staff should select a group of finalists and send those to the judges for final placements. Post winners or all entries on a site such as MySpace that utilizes MP3s.

VARIATIONS

- Consider having the contest be just creative writing, where teens turn in lyrics without music. The contest could also have themed categories, such as heartbreaker songs for Valentine's Day, rap, or duel/fight songs.
- Before the contest begins, invite teens to vote on their opinion of the best and worst lyrics of all time on a blog.
- Pair this contest with an album design cover.
- Host a musical evening where teens could play air guitar, Guitar Hero, Rock Band, or other music video games. Play a song, hand out lyrics, and invite teens to write better ones.
- Invite teens to turn in short music videos that use real songs or their own.

PROMOTION

Rather than flyers, make handouts the size of CD covers and slip them in a display of CDs. Post song lyrics on a poster with CD covers and see if teens can match them.

ART MEDIA MIXER

This is a two-hour event where teens go from station to station trying simple yet fun mediums of art like calligraphy. This one is especially good to test the waters and see if there is enough interest in having an art club like the CREATEens described in chapter 1. This event goes beyond basic crafts to inspire teen artists.

PREPARATION TIME

2 months for publicity, demonstration, and shopping time

LENGTH OF PROGRAM

2 hours

NUMBER OF TEENS

25

SUGGESTED AGE RANGE

Grades 7–10

SHOPPING LIST

Staff can select 4–5 mediums of art for this program. Different options and supplies are listed.

CHARCOAL DRAWING

- ❑ Cloth crumpled up on which objects to draw are placed
- ❑ Charcoal for drawing
- ❑ Drawing paper

SPLATTER PAINT

- ❑ Plastic tarps
- ❑ Brushes of various sizes
- ❑ Tempura paint
- ❑ Tarp for floor
- ❑ Large paper

MOSAIC

- ❑ Grout
- ❑ Picture frames from craft store that mosaic can be glued on
- ❑ Chipped china or plates from thrift stores
- ❑ Craft glue
- ❑ Strong baggies
- ❑ Rubber mallet to break dishes

ORIGAMI

- ❑ Origami paper

CALLIGRAPHY

- ❑ Calligraphy pens
- ❑ Paper

PAPERMAKING

- ❑ Blender
- ❑ Papermaking screen and deckle (craft stores)
- ❑ Styrofoam trays
- ❑ Dried flowers
- ❑ Newspapers and magazines for recycling
- ❑ Container to hold water and pulp—large and flat

SET IT UP

TWO MONTHS BEFORE

Begin researching supplies and directions for all stations. Make lists of library resources for each topic and copy instructions for each. Obtain photos of famous artists' work in each medium, such as Jackson Pollack paintings for splatter paint. Be sure to test all projects ahead of time. Your successful results can be used in displays to attract teens' attention. Consider hiring a local art teacher to help with this program, though it can easily be done by staff. Other library staff may have skills in these areas and be willing to help.

DAY OF PROGRAM

Set up all the stations. Be sure to allow plenty of room for splatter paint.

MAKE IT HAPPEN

As teens enter the room, direct them to a station where they can begin work or where they can wait for a demonstration. The stations for mosaic, splatter painting, and papermaking should be done first because they have to dry.

CHARCOAL DRAWING

Teens here should be encouraged to sample with blending techniques and light and dark shades on a few sheets of paper while drawing the objects on the table.

SPLATTER PAINT

Easy and fun, this one is of course messy. Move furniture out of the way and put down a big tarp or do this one outside. Tempura paint is permanent, but this won't work with watercolors! Teens should get a little paint on their brushes and flick them on the ground toward the paper. One option is to put down a huge piece of butcher paper and just have teens create a big mural for the teen area of the library.

MOSAIC

Use two layers of baggies with a plate or a couple cups in it and break it up with the hammer. Use glue and grout to put pieces around the picture frames.

ORIGAMI

Several options for paper folding from library resources should be provided, or teens could watch a YouTube or short DVD on the subject. Staff should find traditional projects like the crane or try more elaborate monsters and animals to see if teens can do it.

CALLIGRAPHY

Again, several options for this should be available from library resources. Teens should be encouraged to try several sentences in different scripts.

PAPERMAKING

Tear paper into small pieces and soak in the water in a flat pan. Wet paper should then be put in the blender and blended into pulp. The pulp is put back in the flat pan. Put dried flower petals or confetti on top of the pulp. Put the screen and deckle in the pulp per provided instructions with that equipment and then pull it out, shaking side to side.

Let that drain, then flip the screen over onto the Styrofoam tray. Sponge off excess water through the screen and carefully lift the screen off. Let the paper dry.

VARIATIONS

- Post possible projects ahead of time and have teens vote on which mediums they want to sample. They may even give ideas for other projects.
- Do this as an after-school series over a week or once a week, growing it into an art club as described in chapter 1.

PROMOTION

- Make a display featuring some of the projects and the "Art of Reading" booklist from chapter 3.
- Hold a demonstration of one of the projects at a busy time in the library where teens would see it and advertise the program.
- Contact art classes in the area.

12

August

August is both busy and slow. Summer reading ends at the public library, and teens are busy getting ready for school. Although fall school activities often begin in August and some families take last-minute vacations, there may still be time to squeeze in some fun events for teens who do not go on vacations or younger teens without as many activities to return to in the fall.

Community Collaborations is presented here as a possible end-of-summer celebration or a beginning-of-the-school-year initiative. A few ideas are listed for partnership programs. Microwave Madness may be good at any time of year, too, but August is a fun time to teach easy snack making for after-school treats. Library Orienteering will help teens with teamwork and direction in a fun way, skills that will definitely be useful in new school environments.

COMMUNITY COLLABORATIONS

Working with other organizations in the community, although potentially time consuming, can be very gratifying. Possible partners include the park district, the Y, teen centers or counseling centers, schools, and libraries in nearby towns. Working together creates rewarding opportunities to share resources and ideas and reach new groups of teens. Often each agency will discover ways in which the other can help their services, such as a list of online or live tutoring available through the library that would help an after-school drop-in center for teens. It is always good for school media staff to be visible in an age of cuts and staff reductions, as well as for public library staff. It does involve diplomacy and patience while each agency adjusts to the parameters and rules of the other. This section outlines a few fun activities that can be coordinated across agencies, including running a clothing/book/food/school supply drive, a Moveable Feast, or gaming tournaments.

A good way to open the door to a partnership program is by having library staff help with time and materials at another agency's big event. Hold a school open house or a teen BBQ or invite agencies to come to the library for a National Library Week celebration. Often this will involve tables with handouts and materials, but library staff could bring dessert and drawing prizes to a teen drop-in center or something similar that would enhance the event.

After any partnership activity, it is important to write a positive follow-up note or to call to express appreciation for their cooperation—no matter how it went!

PREPARATION TIME

Varies by event; staff need to discover the lead time needed for partner agency's publicity

LENGTH OF PROGRAM

Varies by event; most take place over 2 hours or in contest form over a month

NUMBER OF TEENS

No limit

SUGGESTED AGE RANGE

Grades 6–10

SHOPPING LIST

CLOTHING, FOOD, BOOK, OR SCHOOL SUPPLY DRIVE
- ❑ Several cardboard boxes
- ❑ Paint
- ❑ Brushes

MOVEABLE FEAST
- ❑ Food for assigned section of course, such as dessert

GAMING TOURNAMENTS
- ❑ Agreed gaming platform and game for each location
- ❑ Gaming platform and screens set up for LAN of 8 or more

☐ Snacks for the night of the event

☐ Laptop

SET IT UP

TWO MONTHS BEFORE

- Invite one or more agencies to partner on a project or program. Meet with staff from the other agency, bringing teens from each if possible. Collect handouts from that agency and learn as much as possible about their facility.
- Set up another meeting prior to the event if necessary to work on supplies, parameters if it is a drive, or other details.

ONE WEEK BEFORE

Contact the agency to go over final details, such as number of teens registered or how materials for a drive will be picked up.

MAKE IT HAPPEN

CLOTHING, FOOD, BOOK, OR SCHOOL SUPPLY DRIVE

Ask teens to help identify a need in the community. This could be a clothing drive, food drive, book drive for a school or day care, or school supply drive. Have teens at each participating agency decorate boxes to collect the materials and be responsible for emptying the boxes and bringing the collected items to the selected place in need. The library could sponsor a pizza party for the agency that collects the most materials or a large party for the teens at all participating agencies.

MOVEABLE FEAST

Organize a Meet the Teen community function with a course at each location or on different nights during a Celebrate Teen Week. The Schaumburg Township District Library participates in a township Teen Appreciation Week each August run by the Township Spectrum Youth and Family Center with handouts and events. A Moveable Feast may require a bus to take teens to different places if it is held on the same night, where teens would have appetizers at one location, sandwiches or pizza at another, and dessert at yet another.

GAMING TOURNAMENTS

Coordinate each agency to host a tournament on the same night, with the same game. Post winning scores on a blog or wiki as they are turned in. Have each location award a prize to the winner, with a grand prize for the night's overall winner or host a master tournament for all winners on another night.

Or offer gaming nights at each agency on different nights with mini tournaments, encouraging teens to best the best scores.

VARIATIONS

While a few variations for programs were provided in this section, some of these ideas could be applied to different departments or branches within the library system or school. Clubs at a school could compete in a food drive, or a Moveable Feast could be offered to feature different departments in a public library.

PROMOTION

- Another benefit of partnerships is more promotion because each agency promotes events. Ensure that all information is correctly spelled and listed for each agency in all publicity. Assign one agency to make flyers or one staff member or teen to design posters and copy for flyers at all locations to save time.
- Teens that frequent both locations will be surprised and pleased at the events featuring both staff and will tell friends ahead of time at one agency that they are familiar with the other.
- Staff should ensure that boards and supervisors know about the collaboration. Community papers would likely also be interested in running a release, as it would cover more than one agency.

MICROWAVE MADNESS

Who doesn't want to learn how to make some easy, delicious snacks? In a Microwave Madness class teens can create some simple treats with their own creative touch. While many school and public libraries may not have a kitchen for a cooking program, many will have a microwave at least in staff areas that could perhaps be moved for this event.

PREPARATION TIME

4 hours for shopping and setup

LENGTH OF PROGRAM

1 hour

NUMBER OF TEENS

25

SUGGESTED AGE RANGE

Grades 6–12

SHOPPING LIST

- ❑ Microwaveable plates or bowls
- ❑ Cups or bottled water
- ❑ Plastic or permanent eating utensils

BAKED APPLES
- ❑ 2–3 types of apples, sliced with peels
- ❑ Shredded cheddar
- ❑ Raisins
- ❑ Cinnamon
- ❑ Nutmeg
- ❑ Margarine

- ❑ Brown sugar
- ❑ White sugar
- ❑ Optional: caramel candies or caramel apple wrap, chocolate chips, butterscotch chips, seasonal sprinkles

NACHOS
- ❑ 2–3 types of corn chips
- ❑ 2–3 types of cheese, including Velveeta
- ❑ Canned chili
- ❑ Refried beans
- ❑ Green and black olives
- ❑ 2–3 types of salsa
- ❑ Chili powder
- ❑ Green chili peppers
- ❑ Hot sauce

HAYSTACKS
- ❑ Chocolate chips
- ❑ Butterscotch chips
- ❑ Peanut butter
- ❑ Pretzel sticks
- ❑ Chow mein noodles
- ❑ Mini marshmallows
- ❑ M&Ms
- ❑ Raisins

SET IT UP

TWO MONTHS BEFORE

- Plan menu and type of snacks for the event.
- Begin publicity, targeting grocery stores, cooking classes at the park district, and cafés in particular.

ONE WEEK BEFORE

Shop for food and paper goods. Test out recipes and take digital photos. While it may seem like a good idea to do this well in advance and then to have photos for printed publicity, shopping closer to the date ensures that the same grocery products will be available. For example, fall sprinkles for the haystacks or apples will not be available all the time, or particular types of apples either.

DAY OF PROGRAM

Set up each table for four teens by placing a few of each ingredient on each table for the first recipe. Prep the foods as needed, such as slicing the apples. Put out water on each table for palate cleansing.

MAKE IT HAPPEN

As the teens come in, remind them to wash their hands. Review the three recipes. Each table will make one concoction per set of ingredients.

BAKED APPLES

Teens should start by putting several apple slices in a microwaveable bowl. Then they may add some brown or white sugar, raisins, cinnamon, nutmeg, or melted margarine drizzled over the apples. If they choose to include cheese, they will add it after the initial "baking" of the apples.

Each group should microwave their apples for about 3–3½ minutes until tender. (Different apples may have different cooking times.) If teens choose to include cheese, they should add it now and zap it again for another 15 seconds.

Back at their table, teens can rate the flavor combination they chose. They are welcome to make this one more time with a different combination. For apples, a dessert-type apple could be made by melting caramel candies in the microwave, or caramel apple wraps or chocolate/butterscotch chips, and drizzling them over the apples with seasonal sprinkles such as fall leaves.

NACHOS

This is the easiest of the three and teens can try different types of chips, salsa toppings, cheese, black and green olives, refried beans, canned chili, Velveeta, chili peppers, or chili powder. This should be microwaved for no more than 1 minute or just until the cheese bubbles.

Again, teens should vote on the flavor combination and try again.

HAYSTACKS

Teens first need to microwave chocolate or butterscotch chips and ¼ cup peanut butter for 45 seconds, until it can be easily stirred. Then teens have the choice of using pretzels, chow mein noodles, mini marshmallows, M&Ms, raisins, and the like to form the stacks.

Make copies of the recipes each table used that were teen favorites and hand them out at the end.

VARIATIONS

- Iron Chef Microwave Style: Invite each table to be judged by a predetermined panel after each creation on presentation and taste.
- Healthy Snacks: Teens could easily be presented with only healthier choices to make, including trail mix–type healthy haystacks, popcorn balls with better choices, etc.

PROMOTION

- Hand out a sample recipe for the baked apples with the program information on the back at teen programs before the event. Put up posters in grocery stores, cafés, etc., where teens might be eating or want to be eating!
- Use the "Fabulous Food" booklist from chapter 3 and set up a display with fake food or ingredients to get attention.
- Wear an apron while working at the desk (or hang one up) on the days before the event to boost questions or registration. Teens may not ask outright, but they will notice.

LIBRARY ORIENTEERING

S cavenger hunts are great ways to learn about the community where a teen spends their time. School-wide scavenger hunts can help teens learn about a new school and community; neighborhood hunts enable teens to learn more about the world around them and the resources available in their community.

PREPARATION TIME

1–2 months for planning
2 hours to set up

LENGTH OF PROGRAM

From 1 hour to an entire day, depending on the number of clues and where they are hidden

NUMBER OF TEENS

As many as possible

SUGGESTED AGE RANGE

Grades 9–12

SHOPPING LIST

❑ Clues (choose library or themed items to hide)
❑ Snacks (make a trail mix with nuts, M&Ms, chocolate chips, raisins, dried fruit, marshmallows, dry cereal, etc.)
❑ Baggies
❑ Bottled water
❑ Prizes
❑ Compasses or GPS/geocache equipment
❑ Enough different-colored bandanas so that you have a different color for each team; you may provide one for each team leader or one for each teammate

SET IT UP

Map out the area where you want to place your clues. Each clue should lead to the next one and so on until teens are led to the meeting place at the end of the hunt where you will greet them with treats and prizes! Decide before you start if you are going to use traditional directions or GPS coordinates for each clue. Whichever you choose, write each clue so that the information gives the directions to the next clue. Before you hide clues around your library or school, be sure to ask permission from coworkers, teachers, or others especially if you will be disrupting their space during the scavenger hunt.

MAKE IT HAPPEN

Mix all the snack items together to make a trail mix. Bag up 1-cup portions in individual baggies to hand out with bottled water and clues.

Divide teens into teams paired with an adult. Let each team decide on their name and choose a colored bandana. Hand each team their beginning clue and let them set off on their way.

VARIATIONS

This program could be held at a variety of locations that tie in with a summer theme or to teach teens about several places in their community.

PROMOTION

Print flyers on map backgrounds or even use old maps and Sharpies. Use clever clues to advertise the program.

13

September

As the school year starts, teens have a lot going on, from sports to clubs to homework. Many will be coming to the library for homework or to hang out after school. Public libraries will also not want to lose the momentum from summer programming. So while September programs need to be low-key and easy for both students and staff, they can still keep teens interested in the library. School and public libraries may want to begin programs in September that will conclude in October during Teen Read Week or host some simple back-to-school events. Monthly clubs may be back to their regular schedule in September, too. A Comic Contest may inspire creativity and gauge interest in a possible new club, as will Anime Viewers. When assignments start, Science Fair Fun: From Fabulous Exhibits to Flops takes a humorous approach to showing teens the ins and outs of creating successful science experiments.

COMIC CONTEST

Lots of different types of contests are featured in this book. Even if a few teens participate in a contest the first time it is offered, it is a good way to find out what types of things local teens are interested in. It is also another chance to reward excellence for creative teens who may not have as many other opportunities as teens who ace academics or sports do. A Comic Contest may catch the eye of a teen who is neither a great writer nor artist, but who has ideas for a funny or dramatic scene that can be captured in a few boxes. This is not to say that designing comics is easy, but that it may seem less daunting to a teen who is not confident than a writing contest or an art contest by itself would be.

PREPARATION TIME

2 hours for publicity, shopping

LENGTH OF PROGRAM

1 month for contest to run

NUMBER OF TEENS

No limit

SUGGESTED AGE RANGE

Grades 6–10

SHOPPING LIST

❑ Prizes such as gift certificates to a local comic shop, books on comic history, art supplies, or a computer program on designing comics

SET IT UP

TWO MONTHS BEFORE

During summer events at the public library, begin handing out forms with four boxes for the comics. (A sample form is provided in the appendix.) All entrants will work off the same form, with felt tip and/or color, depending if the library wants to scan the entries in after the event. At the school library, these can be put out at the beginning of the school year or put out with registration materials to get teens thinking.

Choose judges and send them information about the contest. They can be a panel of adults and teens, local experts, or simply people who enjoy reading comics. A shy teen who loves reading them but who is not willing to enter a contest may be thrilled to judge. Consider offering judges money off fines if they are teens or a token gift such as an autographed book or poster.

ONE WEEK BEFORE

Forms should be sent to schools or targeted classrooms the week before the contest begins to promote interest.

MAKE IT HAPPEN

When forms are turned in during the contest period, keep track of them in a database. At the end of the contest period, photocopy those that staff feel should be finalists before sending them on to the judges for final choices of winners. Consider printing all entries in a mini library 'zine for patrons to enjoy reading or scanning them in for online enjoyment.

Send letters to those teens who did not win to encourage them to participate in future contests. Award prizes to winners.

VARIATIONS

- A comic contest on a theme may help give teens direction, such as a humorous comic, a library-themed comic, or a reading-themed one. Another theme idea is to invite teens to design their own superhero and outline his/her adventures. Teens could also be invited to tell in a story what happens next in a particular scenario or after a provided first square in a strip.
- Staff could have a comic creation program with a local artist or writer where teens would work on their entries during the event.
- Prizes could be awarded for different skills, such as most creative, best story depicted in four panels, best dialogue, or funniest characters, to attract different teens to the contest.
- Online comic contests that could be created with a program on the library computers is another variation.

PROMOTION

Links to online comics such as Unshelved should be prominently displayed on library teen sites. Book and media displays in the library could feature comic books, comic history, comic design, and art instruction.

ANIME VIEWERS

It can be expensive to start purchasing a new graphic novel series or DVD anime series that patrons then do not keep checking out. Anime Viewers is a movie night for anime fans where they can see newly available series at the library. Libraries will need the movie license to show films from particular companies. If a library is not able to show the movies due to the license, new anime books or video games could be featured instead. This program features the movies. While it may seem like a simple program—inviting staff to show anime episodes—it could turn into a monthly club or utilize teen input for new directions for the collection.

PREPARATION TIME

1 hour for publicity and shopping

LENGTH OF PROGRAM

90 minutes

NUMBER OF TEENS

50

SUGGESTED AGE RANGE

Grades 7–12

SHOPPING LIST

- ❑ DVDs to show approximately three 30-minute shows
- ❑ Snacks such as Pocky, popcorn

SET IT UP

ONE MONTH BEFORE

Advertise that "Anime Viewers is coming" on online sources and give teens a chance to vote on what to watch that evening. Offer a selection of five 30-minute shows from different series covered by your viewing license and let teens choose. Space should be allowed for suggestions for movies in case on the night of the event the chosen movies bomb with the group and something else is needed to fill the time.

Teens should not be able to vote without registering so that staff will have contact information for publicity. This will also reduce the likelihood that people will vote more than once.

DAY OF PROGRAM

Ensure that equipment is set up and functioning. Set out snacks.

MAKE IT HAPPEN

Show the movies without disclosing their titles, basing their sequence on the number of votes they received, from the third most popular to the first, so that teens may stay to see what won. If a particular movie does not hold teens' interest, offer to stop it and move on. There is no sense in forcing the group to view a movie they don't enjoy.

VARIATIONS

- Cosplay: Invite teens to come dressed as a favorite book or movie anime character for chances to win prizes.
- Books: Put out possible new series and let teens browse during a particular time or between movie showings. They can then vote on what ones to purchase for the library or not.
- Show a longer anime title rather than several short episodes.
- Offer themed anime or manga evenings, such as super schoolgirls, romantic flicks, American anime, etc.
- Consider offering the Anime Viewers every time there is a day off from school or early dismissal day. Then teens will be accustomed to the voting and looking for the event to happen.

PROMOTION

- Anime events promote themselves to the dedicated teens who enjoy them. To help spread the word, distribute theater-style ticket handouts with information about the evening.
- Put the covers of the five possible movies up on posters in the library, school, and local comic and bookstores.
- Have links to the voting for the movies to be shown on the library website.

SCIENCE FAIR FUN

FROM FABULOUS EXHIBITS TO FLOPS

For some teens, science fair season can be a great time to explore the sciences and dream up creative projects to wow judges; for nonscience lovers this can be a stressful time of year if they are struggling to come up with the perfect project. Hosting a science fair night at your library will likely be appealing to both groups. You can enlist the help of teens and have them show off previous projects that worked and bring in some experts to help them broaden their horizons and devise creative crowd-pleasing science fair projects.

PREPARATION TIME

1 month

LENGTH OF PROGRAM

90 minutes

NUMBER OF TEENS

Up to 50

SUGGESTED AGE RANGE

Grades 6–10

SHOPPING LIST

Note: Refreshments and supplies will cost about $50 (per 50 attendees).

- ❑ Cookies
- ❑ Punch
- ❑ Ice
- ❑ Tablecloths, napkins, plates, cups
- ❑ Pens and pencils
- ❑ Name tags
- ❑ Donated items for door prizes and giveaways

SET IT UP

ONE MONTH BEFORE

- Invite guest speakers. Start out by visiting with teens in your library and soliciting those who are yearly participants in science fairs sponsored by schools, districts, cities, or counties. Invite them to participate either by displaying winning projects or by making a presentation to a group or audience about how they chose their project and the process they went through. Contact a local high school or university science department to send a representative to discuss experiments and presentations. It is also a good idea to invite previous judges to talk about what makes a winning presentation.

- Clear any science demonstrations with administrative staff, especially ones that involve dry ice, chemicals, smoke, loud noises, etc. Set out publicity as early as possible along with science book displays and bookmarks to get teens interested. Check with schools to see which ones sponsor science fairs. Also check with city, county, or regional offices in your area to find out if teens have options for advancing their projects after the school fairs.
- Contact area businesses and solicit donations or begin shopping for prizes to give to teens who participate by showing their projects or presenting to audiences and for door prizes for the teens attending.

MAKE IT HAPPEN

1. Set up refreshments and tables with chairs for trivia game participants. Set up tables for projects to be displayed on or around the perimeter of the room, and then set up chairs in the middle for the audience. When you greet teens at the door, have them fill out drawing slips for door prizes to be given away at the end of the program.

2. Try to find sample projects for several different sciences, such as biology and life sciences, chemistry, and cooking and consumer sciences. Remember, the wider the variety of exhibits, the better. It is really helpful to have judges for all the different levels teens in your area can participate in. Schools judge differently from city or county events, and the state level usually has their own rules.

3. Invite some of the participants to demonstrate easy mistakes to make while putting together science fair projects—or flops to avoid. Make sure some are visual and humorous enough to be memorable for audience members.

VARIATIONS

Have hands-on experiments ready for the teens to practice. Have a display demonstrating the scientific procedures and how to document the procedures used in the experiment. Also, spend some time discussing the differences between a scientific demonstration and a science experiment.

PROMOTION

Use blue ribbons, trophies, medals, etc., to decorate the library in a science fair theme. Display science books and make bookmarks listing books and information for the event. Make flyers with all of the information about the event and share them with schools, libraries, or other agencies in the area. Partner with school or public libraries in the area to promote the program.

October

The school year is in full swing, and many fall activities keep teens busy, from sports to homecoming to college prep tests. Still, some younger teens may be at loose ends. Older teens who are not as interested in school activities may be looking for something fun and different to do as well. YALSA's Teen Read Week is always in October, and libraries should always promote any reading celebration they can! A Totally Teen Read-in during that week may appeal to younger teens after hours. In communities where busily scheduled teens have little time to get to the library, a simple contest like the Mangamania Reviewing Contest may be the way to go. Spooky programs are always a draw with teens, and October is a good time to offer something along those lines, such as Haunted Gingerbread Houses.

TOTALLY TEEN READ-IN

Not ready for a lock-in? Try a read-in! This easy program can be done in a number of ways, but would be fun as a simple after-hours event if staff are not yet ready to attempt a complicated lock-in. This is also a good event for school media centers.

PREPARATION TIME

2 hours for shopping and publicity

LENGTH OF PROGRAM

3–4 hours

NUMBER OF TEENS

25

SUGGESTED AGE RANGE

Grades 6–10

SHOPPING LIST

❑ Snacks for starving readers
❑ Incentives for attendance such as pencils and bookmarks
❑ Prizes for drawings such as books and inexpensive fast-food coupons

SET IT UP

TWO MONTHS BEFORE

Consider planning the read-in to coincide with Teen Read Week, National Library Week, or other literary celebrations. Begin marketing the event with notices in library publications, online posts, announcements, and posters. Registration will be needed for this event, so allow plenty of time for patrons to find out about it.

No one wants to sit for enforced quiet reading for 3 to 4 hours, so plan other activities to break it up. Perhaps there will be a quiet reading station with comfortable chairs, a station for snacks, and another for a craft, movie, or electronic game to change the pace. Teens may bring their own reading material or choose from a cart or table of enticing selections set up by staff.

Rather than requiring teens to read for a particular length of time as during the school day, plan to mark how many pages are read toward a goal for inspiration. If the teens reach a particular number of pages during the event, plan a prize. For example, if teens read 500 pages during the evening, posters to that effect with teen names will be posted, or each teen who attended will receive a token gift, or another reward program will be planned. Advertise this plan and goal ahead of time so teens plan to read at the event.

TWO WEEKS BEFORE

Gather supplies needed for planned stations and shop for food and prizes. Send out reminders to teens who are registered or to the general teen mailing list to garner more responses. If parental permission forms are required for after-hours events, ensure that this is done.

Set up the stations and snacks.

MAKE IT HAPPEN

1. As teens arrive, check them in and direct them to the different stations. Invite the ones going to the reading area to select a book and register it, along with the number of pages read. At points throughout the evening, invite teens to switch stations or take a break from reading if they choose to stay there the entire time.

2. Hold any drawings close to the ending time.

VARIATIONS

- Host a read-in during library hours on a Saturday. Have teens come and check in to a particular room or area of the library and check out with number of pages or minutes read when they are through. Offer snacks. Give each who comes a raffle slip or small incentive.
- Host a virtual read-in over a particular time. Teens can register online during a set day or week with what they read, how many pages they read, or how many minutes.
- Host a read-in for audiobooks where teens can compare notes about audiobooks online throughout a month.
- Host a themed read-in. Invite teens to come read titles from a specified list or theme or graphic novels with themed incentives.
- Hold a read-in at another agency or at a local bookstore.

PROMOTION

- Teachers in junior and senior high schools may be willing to offer extra credit for participation in the read-in if contacted early enough. Create simple forms for teachers to hand out for students to get signed and return after the event, or simply let teachers know which teens came. Ask teens what school and which teacher mentioned extra credit when they came for accuracy.
- Put bookmarks in teen materials beginning six weeks before the event to catch the notice of teens who just come in the library for books and perhaps not to participate in other programs or who may not be getting the mailings.

MANGAMANIA REVIEWING CONTEST

Everyone has seen teens with stacks of graphic novels in the library, going through them like candy. It is impossible for library staff to keep up with reading all the new graphic novels and series for readers' advisory. Combine these two areas with a simple Managamania Reviewing Contest. Invite teens to turn in as many reviews as possible for prizes during October. Collect the reviews and post them online or on a bulletin board to offer another readers' advisory tool and inspire even more readers. A contest such as this offers legitimacy to reading graphic novels for adults who may not consider it as worthwhile as reading other types of books.

PREPARATION TIME

1 hour for publicity

LENGTH OF PROGRAM

1 month for contest to run

NUMBER OF TEENS

No limit

SUGGESTED AGE RANGE

Grades 6–12

SHOPPING LIST

❑ Prizes for winners, possibly including gift certificates to local comic bookstores or larger bookstores that carry manga

SET IT UP

SIX WEEKS BEFORE

- Choose parameters for the contest. Will prizes be given to the teens who turn in the most forms during the month of the contest? Will the teens need to read the titles during October to count? Will there be limits to the number of books read or number of books per series? Keep the contest with as few limits as possible while still making it inviting to teens at all levels of readership. Consider offering some drawings from all the slips for smaller prizes such as a book or journal so those who can turn in only a few slips still have inspiration.
- Put up posters advertising the contest with rules in the library, in classrooms, and at the local comic store or general bookstore.
- Organize the online component of the program if applicable.

TWO WEEKS BEFORE

Make many copies of book review forms for teens to fill out. It is possible that a few fans will submit as many as a hundred of these. Forms should not be too difficult, yet should ensure that the teen read the book and that the form may inspire other teens to read the book. Consider asking a few questions, but forms should not be longer than half a page in length to avoid seeming like a school assignment or book report. A few questions also keep the contest fair, so one teen could not turn in hundreds with a two-word review. Possible questions include the following.

- Please provide a three-sentence summary of the plot.
- Is this title like any other series? Why?
- How did you feel about the book?
- What are some of your favorite graphic novel series?

Forms for any contest in the library should include a box asking teens if they would like more information about library services. Teens who answer yes and provide an e-mail address can be put on the mailing list for more promotions. The form should ask for contact information that can be cut off. For example, the name, phone number, and e-mail address could be cut off so the form could be stapled to a bulletin board or poster for patrons to peruse.

Consider sending forms to schools or public library partners to hand out to teens. Offer other sites an envelope to collect them to provide easier participation in the event. All sites could begin handing out forms early, as long as it is clear that none will be collected until the first day of the program.

MAKE IT HAPPEN

During the entire month when teens may turn in forms, staff need to be sure to keep supplying the forms if they run out. Respond to online form entries so teens know staff received them. At the end of the month, count the total reviews and award prizes to the three teens who turned in the most. Draw names if desired of a few teens from the entire collection pool.

Post the names of the winners with numbers of reviews turned in. Collect and post the reviews for staff and patrons to use for readers' advisory.

VARIATIONS

- This contest could run for just one or two weeks.
- While this program is designed to promote graphic novel reading, it could easily be adapted to promote reading through media such as audiobooks or themed lists such as state award titles, nonfiction, books from selection lists, and more.
- This program could also be used in the summer along with summer reading for those teens who finish that program quickly and want more to do.
- Collection of reviews with prizes is something that could be done throughout the year. Chapter 2 outlines several ongoing reading promotions such as this.

PROMOTION

- Post a chart in the library or online indicating how many reviews are being turned in throughout the program to keep interest and momentum going.
- Post reviews on a blog or website or in the library to inspire more teens to write.
- Send forms out over e-mail halfway through the program to remind teens to turn them in.

HAUNTED GINGERBREAD HOUSES

People of all ages like making gingerbread houses, but there is something uniquely appealing to teens about making haunted gingerbread houses for Halloween. Perhaps it is the black frosting or the lack of cuteness. This is definitely a messy program, but memorable for all involved!

PREPARATION TIME

2 weeks

LENGTH OF PROGRAM

1 hour

NUMBER OF TEENS

20

SUGGESTED AGE RANGE

Grades 7–12

SHOPPING LIST

❏ Kits for making haunted gingerbread houses or undecorated gingerbread houses (many discount store bakeries have these for several holidays)

Or, if not using kits:

❏ 20 small, used milk cartons, rinsed out with bleach water and thoroughly dried, with tops stapled shut

❏ 7 boxes of graham crackers

❏ Multiple jars of chocolate frosting to hold the structures together

❏ Tubes of edible decorating gel in black, orange, red

❏ Strong paper plates for platforms

For both kits and milk cartons:

❏ Candy for decorations, including licorice, candy corn, and pumpkins; cake decorations such as ghosts or witches' hats, M&Ms, gumdrops, and the like

❏ Coconut

❏ Baggies to dye coconut

❏ Plastic wrap for covering projects to take home

❏ Small plates or bowls for decorations

❏ Paper towels

SET IT UP

ONE MONTH BEFORE

- Advertise the Haunted Gingerbread Houses program through online posts and posters. Consider contacting food science and art teachers as well.

- Consider charging a small fee to go toward supplies and to ensure that registered teens attend, as this may be a popular event.
- If using kits, begin scouting fall sales in September at craft stores and discount stores. Or call bakeries to check their prices for undecorated houses.
- If you plan to use milk cartons, contact a school to see if they can collect about 25 to 30 cartons. The extra are in case a teen wants a multiple-carton structure or something irreparable happens to one house.

ONE WEEK BEFORE

If using kits, check each one to see if advance construction and drying time of the houses is needed. Also check to see if reconstituting is required for frostings in powdered form. If using cartons, get them rinsed with bleach water, dried, and stapled closed.

DAY OF PROGRAM

Play spooky music to set mood. Cover all tables with newspaper or vinyl covers. Set milk cartons and paper plates at each place. Put decorations in bowls or plates on a central table or a few on each table for teens to use. Do not put all candies out at once, or many will be eaten and there may not be enough to decorate!

MAKE IT HAPPEN

Once started, this program needs little direction. Teens will go off and create. Staff may be needed to supply more candies or to stop teens from eating all the black gel frosting, but the fewer suggestions from staff on the houses, the better. Make sure to take plenty of photos or short videos for library promotions.

VARIATIONS

- A simpler form of this program would be to decorate cookies or brownies as ghosts, monsters, etc.
- Another idea is to make cardboard shoe boxes into haunted dioramas or haunted houses covered with paper and glued-on decorations.
- This program could be held at different times of year for teens to create a gingerbread dream house or gingerbread McMansion. A contest could be held for teens to sign up for kits and turn them in to the library for display and voting.
- Staff from a local bakery or craft store could come in to demonstrate advanced decorating tips.

PROMOTION

- Posters and flyers should include pictures where possible to attract attention. A sample product is another good way to help teens remember to sign up for this event. If it is popular enough to host two sessions, that may be a good idea rather than a large, unmanageable crowd.
- Craft stores where kits were purchased may also help promote the event.

15

November

Definitely November is a busy month for teens with sports finals, days off for Thanksgiving, and big assignments due. A few fairly simple programs that may work well during this time include a short Stellar Scene Contest, which could be held with different media. Creative Carding could be timely for Veterans' Day, when teens could make cards for soldiers who need to travel throughout the holidays. Moneyene is an educational program with fun, interactive elements that will keep the college application process in teens' minds.

STELLAR SCENE CONTEST

Picture a favorite movie. What is a memorable scene? What one-liners pop into your mind instantly from movies? What is it about that moment that is captured so well? Invite teens to answer those questions with a Stellar Scene Contest. This differs from the Magic Moment Writing Challenge in the May chapter with dialogue and stage directions. The scene provides much of the tension and drama of an entire plot. Teens can write a Stellar Scene or they could capture it in a short movie. This program will feature the written contest, with the movie option listed under "Variations."

PREPARATION TIME

2 hours for shopping, publicity, and judging

LENGTH OF PROGRAM

1 month

NUMBER OF TEENS

25 (suggested limit)

SUGGESTED AGE RANGE

Grades 7–12

SHOPPING LIST

Prizes such as gift certificates to local bookstores or multimedia stores

SET IT UP

TWO MONTHS BEFORE

- Contact possible judges for the event. These may include high school and community college film or creative writing teachers or theater experts. Judges will evaluate the finalists chosen by the library staff and determine the winners.
- Begin promotion on all media levels with posts online, information sent to schools, and flyers tucked in teen movie cases in the library.
- Distribute forms for teens to attach to their scenes, with rules such as no more than two pages in length and highlighting judging categories.

MAKE IT HAPPEN

1. As the entries come in, keep them in a database. Read through them as they come in, as many may be submitted at the last minute. Put some aside that may be finalists.

2. When all entries are in, send the final ten to judges to rank, along with a suggested scoring system that will grade on creativity, setting, plot, suspense, or similar topics. Do not be discouraged if only a few teens enter the program during the first year it is offered. If fewer than five enter, give awards to the top one and honorable mention to either one or two others or the rest of them.

3. Prepare letters for teens who will not win or place that are encouraging in tone. A teen discouraged from one contest may be discouraged from writing again. Invite them to library events highlighting movies or creative writing.

4. When the judges return their results, send letters and prizes to the top scorers. Publish the scenes online at the library, where possible, or in print to hand out at the library and in the school media centers. Send letters to all teens who entered and did not win. Send thank-you letters to teachers who turned in scenes as class projects and possibly also a book or other small reward.

VARIATIONS

- If there is a lot of interest in the program, consider splitting it into junior and senior high categories or subject topics such as cliff-hangers, horror, or romance.
- A Winner's Night could be held to have teens act out the scenes for an audience. Those could be filmed to post online and to help promote the contest the next year.
- Make the contest for short movies rather than screenplays. Show the movies on library websites; use them for promotion the next year. Rules for this variation could include making scenes no more than 2 minutes.
- Host a program featuring memorable teen movie scenes to kick off the contest. Teens could write in ahead of time with their favorite scenes or staff could choose some.

PROMOTION

- Show or read short scenes at teen programs the entire month before the contest as a mini commercial for the event.
- Having the contest limited to the first twenty-five entries may make it seem more exclusive and appealing, heightening response.

CREATIVE CARDING

Card giving may be a dying social activity, but crafty teens will enjoy sharing them again when you show them how to turn tired old school cards into creative cool ones. DIY cards are a great craft idea for almost any occasion. This can be a long-term activity of many steps completed over a monthly period while you make your own recycled paper, or this can be a shorter activity made from recycled cards cut up and glued into great new cards to send to friends and loved ones. Card making can also make a wonderful passive program. Old cards and supplies can be left out on tables, and instead of doodling teens can create their own cards any time.

PREPARATION TIME

- 1 month minimum to gather used cards and gift wrap
- 60 minutes to set out snacks and set up for the program

LENGTH OF PROGRAM

60 minutes

NUMBER OF TEENS

150

SUGGESTED AGE RANGE

Grades 7–12

SHOPPING LIST

- ❏ Do not purchase, but collect old cards, envelopes, and gift wrap from staff and friends
- ❏ Unfrosted cupcakes (1 or 2 for each participant)
- ❏ Vanilla or chocolate frosting
- ❏ Holiday-themed candy shapes
- ❏ Tacky glue
- ❏ Scissors
- ❏ Poster or watercolor paint
- ❏ Glitter

SET IT UP

TWO MONTHS BEFORE

Begin collecting used cards and materials. Set out a box in the staff room and ask staff to donate materials as they perform seasonal cleaning projects or get ready for upcoming holidays.

TWO WEEKS BEFORE

Sort through collected cards, envelopes, and gift wrap and create sample cards. Decide on a theme (specific holiday, colors, animals, etc.). If desired, have teens choose a group to send or donate completed cards to.

DAY OF PROGRAM

Set out materials and snacks. Make sure to place newspaper or tarps underneath the tables to catch small scraps and glitter.

MAKE IT HAPPEN

The setup is the hard part. Once all of the materials have been set out, turn teens loose and allow them enough space to use their own creativity to create the cards they choose. Because some teens may not be familiar with giving/receiving greeting cards, it might be a good idea to have some samples of cards or a list of writing prompts that teens can copy from.

Once the cards are completed and have had sufficient drying time, allow teens to choose appropriate-sized envelopes that can either be left plain or decorated.

VARIATIONS

- This can be an awesome craft if you make your own paper, but that is a long process and can be extremely messy. Instructions for papermaking can be found in chapter 11.

- Another variation would be to gather leaves, grasses, and flowers to dry and use to decorate the front of cards. For a personal touch, teens could print digital photos of their family or friends to use.

PROMOTION

When creating library displays and contacting area schools, use samples of the greeting cards you are making to advertise the program. On the front of the card put the main information, the name of the library, the date, and the location; on the inside of the card, add more specific information, snacks provided, materials used; on the back cover add a quick "hope to see you there!"

MONEYENE

In chapter 1 a Money Mavericks club was outlined, but Moneyense is a onetime program designed to deal with some teens' fears about money. Schools may already be providing seminars for families on financial aid for college, but this would be a bit more basic. Topics would include college loans, budgeting, financial goals, and real-life money matters.

PREPARATION TIME

2 months for publicity

LENGTH OF PROGRAM

2 hours

NUMBER OF TEENS

50

SUGGESTED AGE RANGE

Grades 7–12

SHOPPING LIST

❑ Snacks (optional)

SET IT UP

TWO MONTHS BEFORE

- Begin making flyers, bookmarks, displays, etc., as described in the "Promotion" section for this program.
- Research college costs at area institutions, as well as interest rates for college loans from local banks.
- Discover the hiring rates for the library teen positions as well as other area employers. Print the scenarios for teens to work with during the program.

- Gather information on financial terms teens may want to know such as *bonds* and *interest rates.* Also gather information on library financial resources and local scholarships.
- Prepare a printed survey asking teens about which areas of financial issues most concern them, as well as which they and their family are best at handling.

DAY OF PROGRAM

Set up a laptop or desktop computer with Internet access. Have a calculator and Money Goal worksheets available with pencils for teens. The worksheets can be blank sheets of paper.

MAKE IT HAPPEN

When teens sign up or come in, invite them to fill out a survey about money strengths and worries, things they don't understand, things their family does well, or things their family is not so good at concerning finances. As the surveys are returned, make a list of the areas the teens are concerned about and be sure to touch on them during the program or to highlight them whenever possible.

COLLEGE LOANS

First, go over financial terms teens may not be familiar with, like *stocks, bonds, loans,* and *interest.* Write the amount it will cost to attend a local community college full-time as well as an area state school where teens may attend. Calculate with teens how much it would cost to take a loan for the entire cost of a semester including books, room and board, etc., at a 5 percent interest rate by the time they graduate. Now multiply that by 4 and then 8 for a rough estimate of what the cost would be for college with a loan.

Go over resources for area scholarships or financial aid. Staff may want to provide a list of those resources and links online and in print for patrons.

BUDGETING

Ask a teen how much they get paid for their job, or use the hiring rate for a shelver at the library. Figure how much they make per week, subtracting for taxes, etc. Then ask teens what a high-price item they want costs, such as a new guitar or going to the prom. Calculate how many hours of work it would take to pay for that.

MONEY GOALS

How much would teens like to save ideally from their current job or by the time they finish high school? What are regular costs teens have? Use their weekly rate to figure out how much they need to spend on those items, plus save for their high-price item, then save some for college or career school. Ask teens what would happen to the budget if something unexpected comes up and what some of those things might be for them.

No college? Before class, pull area rental ads and show teens how much an apartment costs. List how much a used car plus insurance may cost, then add groceries, utilities, and entertainment to let teens know what they would need to earn.

REAL-LIFE MONEY MATTERS

Discuss the following situations or invite teens to act them out with possible solutions.

> **Drunk Driving.** Factor costs if teens are arrested for drunk driving. Include bail, lawyer fee, insurance increase, transportation while having no license, possible loss of work income, and community service access. Then divide those costs by the hourly wage teens indicated they earn.

Credit Crunch. Everyone says paying off credit cards each month is a good idea, but what happens if you can't? How much does a $50 dress cost with a 3.66 percent monthly interest rate after 3 months with minimum payments of $10? How much at a higher interest rate? What are some ways to pay off debt once it has accrued?

College Choices. What if your top school offers no financial aid while a second choice offers full payment? What are ways to make either one work?

Work Costs. Factor nice clothing costs, transportation, and lunch money for a new position. What are some realistic costs for a new position?

Donations and Charitable Giving. What does tax write-off mean? How can donated goods and giving money to nonprofits help financially?

Stocks and investments. Give information about four companies along with stock history from the last month. Ask teens which they would choose with a $1,000 budget and why.

VARIATIONS

- Resource focus group: Libraries receive grants or desire to improve financial resources at times. Consider holding a teen focus group simply to find out what areas of financial literacy teens are most interested in and how they would go about seeking related information. Would teens like mini movies on the website with skits and scenarios about money? Would they like an online trivia game that would direct them to financial resources? Serve pizza and let teens talk money worries with library solutions.
- Link this program to the job skills workshop and invite area teen employers to come talk about their facilities or set up a booth at a job fair.
- Invite a speaker from local college financial aid offices or banks to talk to teens about saving.
- Grow this program into the Money Mavericks club with enough interest.

PROMOTION

This is the type of program parents may force their teens to attend, but it is important to catch teen attention for it, too.

- Make bookmarks that look like dollar bills on one side, with the program information on the other.
- Put flyers and posters in local banks, as well as in economics or business classrooms.
- Create a display that prominently features the Spending Savvy booklist from chapter 3 and information about the Moneyene program. Catch people's attention by scattering fake money around the display.

16

December

With the holidays and finals approaching and the end of the semester looming, December can become a stressful time of year for some teens. The variety of religions and cultures celebrating major holidays during this month makes it a perfect time to host a Festival of Cultures. What better way to get ready for the onslaught of cheer than by clearing out the clutter and adding some new life to old digs with a program that gives teens tips on redecorating their rooms with a Dream Rooms Design Contest. Fun-to-make seasonal decorations will add to the merriment of the month with Decked-Out Halls.

FESTIVAL OF CULTURES

Fitting in is sometimes hard for teens, and helping them to celebrate who they are and where they come from may help them identify with others in their present and past. Food, music, and fun will make everyone feel at home no matter where they are from and will give teens a chance to show off their most unique qualities.

PREPARATION TIME

2 hours for shopping, plus 2 hours for setup

LENGTH OF PROGRAM

90 minutes

NUMBER OF TEENS

25 (suggested limit)

SUGGESTED AGE RANGE

Grades 7–12

SHOPPING LIST

❑ Prizes and paper goods

SET IT UP

TWO MONTHS BEFORE

Begin signing up participants. When teens register, be sure to get information about either the culture that they most relate to or would most like to learn about. Invite them to bring a favorite family dish to share and to decorate their table with cultural objects they would like to display and teach others about. Encourage teens to share favorite music, dances, and other entertainment.

MAKE IT HAPPEN

Contact local ethnic restaurants about donating prizes or food and beverages to sample during the event. Invite local ethnic performance groups to attend and entertain, but provide enough free time for teens to mingle and socialize.

VARIATIONS

Make the program multigenerational by having teens invite their entire families. Create a trivia quiz for each culture represented and have teens collect the answers at each table they visit. Hand out prizes to the teens who collect the most answers.

PROMOTION

Create flyers in various languages. If you can find someone who accurately speaks another language, advertise in multiple languages.

DREAM ROOMS DESIGN CONTEST

The end of the year can be a perfect time to clean up and clear out the old as we get ready for a new year. Give teens a reason to reevaluate their use of space with a DIY room design contest and tips for turning those boring spaces into fresh places. This is a program that can start small, where teens may design a dream room by cutting out pictures of furnishings from magazines, or you may invite designers and home remodeling experts to give teens hands-on tips for building shelves, painting, etc. If you really want to go all out, partner with local businesses and media outlets to sponsor a contest where teens remodel their own spaces and submit before-and-after photographs for prizes.

PREPARATION TIME

2 hours if doing a small project on paper; up to 2 months if planning an all-out contest

LENGTH OF PROGRAM

60 minutes

NUMBER OF TEENS

150

SUGGESTED AGE RANGE

Grades 7–12

SHOPPING LIST

- ❏ Home-decorating magazines
- ❏ Fabric swatches
- ❏ Wallpaper and paint samples
- ❏ Tacky glue
- ❏ Scissors
- ❏ Poster or watercolor paint
- ❏ Poster board
- ❏ Snacks and beverages
- ❏ Prizes

SET IT UP

If you are doing a smaller program, set out magazines, samples, and craft supplies. Allow teens time to peruse the magazines and samples to create their own dream room collage. Spend time talking about each teen's design and what makes their room comfortable to them.

If you want to step it up a bit, invite remodeling and design professionals to talk to teens about aspects of design. What do colors do to our moods? What patterns can you mix and match? How do you select the correct window coverings? How do you create great storage space in a tight room?

Contact local media and form a committee of judges to judge teen submissions of before-and-after photos for a contest, if that's the route you take. Decide on rules for submissions, deadlines, and criteria for judging as well as prizes and publicity.

MAKE IT HAPPEN

Invite professionals to speak at the beginning of the program. Then give teens plenty of time to look over samples and magazines while they socialize and snack. Allow plenty of room for teens to spread out and create their rooms on poster board. If doing an actual design contest, review rules for submissions, deadlines, etc. Have teens and their parents fill out a permission slip confirming that it is okay for teens to compete in this contest.

VARIATIONS

Try to collect doll furniture and dollhouses and have teens compete to see who can decorate the best room. Leave these on display in the teen area.

PROMOTION

Use fabric and wallpaper samples as backgrounds for flyers. Also, if you have access to doll furniture, set up a display with decorating books and samples to advertise your program.

DECKED-OUT HALLS

Encourage teens to get into the holiday spirit by decorating the teen spaces or classrooms in crazy holiday style. Give teams of teens the freedom to choose their themes or assign them themes but limit their materials. Find different ways to mix it up so that teens are forced to explore their more creative side to produce a comprehensive and winning display design.

PREPARATION TIME

2 months for publicity

LENGTH OF PROGRAM

2 hours

NUMBER OF TEENS

50

SUGGESTED AGE RANGE

Grades 7–12

SHOPPING LIST

❏ Snacks (optional)
❏ Leftover craft supplies
❏ Magazines
❏ Paper

SET IT UP

Decide in advance which areas teens will decorate. Move anything that you do not want decorated or accidentally damaged to a safer place or cover it with a sheet or tarp. Decide on themes or colors and divide teens into teams to give them their room or area assignment.

MAKE IT HAPPEN

When thinking of team assignments, use your leftover craft supplies from the past year to help you create fun and interesting themes. For instance team 1 must use only the color red, team 2 must use only construction paper, and team 3 must use glitter or duct tape. Have the required supplies sorted and ready for the teams to pick up so that they do not waste time and make messes gathering their supplies.

VARIATIONS

You don't have to preselect themes. You can allow teens to create their own themes using the materials you supply.

PROMOTION

Make flyers that match your themes to promote the program.

Epilogue

Wrapping It All Up

THE IDEAS WE have set out in this book are just a jumping-off place to get your own creative juices flowing. You know your teens and your community the best, so you know which programs your teens will enjoy and how to turn those programs into great events for your teens. A few things you will want to remember are to always include teens in the planning process for successful programs, to collaborate and partner whenever you can, and to include books and literature in every program you do for teens.

Involving teens in the planning process is an important aspect of teen programming because it helps fulfill their developmental needs. When we allow teens to help us plan programs we give them a voice in the process. We communicate that we value their opinions and ideas and that what they have to say matters to us. When Kim worked at the Lawrence, Kansas, library she had a vital teen advisory board that helped plan every activity they did. At her current position at the library in Kansas City, she is just now beginning to create that vital force yet again, still soliciting advice from teens through surveys and dialogue as she waits for her teen advisory board to grow.

After Amy ran a teen advisory board for over ten years with staff at the Schaumburg Township District Library in Illinois, they took a break and regrouped into a new, more dynamic group with more of an emphasis on community volunteering. Let teens lead the way in changing services and growing them.

Community collaboration is becoming more and more important as funding becomes more scarce. Look at your community and write down possible agencies to partner and collaborate with. Think outside the box to bring in more partners. In Lawrence, Kim saw an issue with teens getting into trouble downtown on early dismissal days. The businesses were overwhelmed with teens clogging their doors and interrupting the business of paying customers. There were loitering problems, fights, trash; it was becoming quite a mess.

The public library is downtown and wanted to step up and help make the situation better, but the sheer number of teens involved was too much for the staff and budget to handle. Kim called a few friends who also work with teens in social service agencies to see if they could pool resources and create a plan. They ended up with a collaboration of over twenty-six agencies and businesses who took turns planning weekly programs and snacks for teens on early dismissal days. One local business loaned his theater so they would have a space to hold events. Teens from every middle school in the city were invited to sit on an advisory board to give teen input.

This program was such a success that it ran for two years until it finally outgrew itself. While it lasted, it was a wonderful opportunity to show teens what a community that cares for them can do to support its teens.

We hope you will continue to enjoy and learn from the teens it is our privilege to serve.

—Kim Patton and Amy Alessio

Appendix

Sample Handouts

Schaumburg Township District Library

....

Teen Corps Application

Want to make a difference in the library and in the community? Meet over pizza and plan our first service projects. Interested teens in grades 6–10 can fill out applications at the central and branch libraries beginning January 1. All will be accepted, but staff want to know about your interests.

FIRST MEETING!
Wednesday, February 18, 6–7 p.m., Youth Services Classroom

Please print. If you have any questions or need more information, contact Amy Alessio at (847) 923-3191 or Dan Schnepf at (847) 923-3192. Return the completed application to the Readers' Services Desk at the central library or the branch libraries by Monday, February 16.

Name: _____

Address: _____

Phone:_____ E-mail address: _____

School: _____ Grade: _____

Why do you want to volunteer at the library?

_____

_____

_____

What projects or causes would you like to see the Teen Corps support?

_____

_____

_____

The Teen Corps meets for 1 hour each month. Can you commit to meeting 1 hour a month during February, March, April, and May and one summer meeting? _____Yes_____No

Teen Corps members may also volunteer at the library at other times with tasks or running programs. Would you be willing to do this? _____Yes _____No

Please list some of your favorite activities and interests.

_____

_____

_____

What's missing at the library? Are there books, graphic novels, music, or games that you think should be available at the library? If so, can you list some examples?

_____

_____

What do you like about the library?

_____

_____

Schaumburg Township District Library
130 S. Roselle Rd. | Schaumburg, IL 60193 | (847) 985-4000 | www.stdl.org
Hoffman Estates Branch | 1550 Hassell Rd. | Hoffman Estates, IL 60169 | (847) 885-3511
Hanover Park Branch | 1266 Irving Park Rd. | Hanover Park, IL 60133 | (630) 372-7800

Schaumburg Township District Library

....

Comic Contest
July 1–31

TEENS IN GRADES 6–12

Design a cartoon for a chance to win a Borders gift certificate! Make your most embarrassing moment into a cartoon. Panels should show a story with a beginning, a middle, and an end. Winners will be displayed in the library during Teen Appreciation Week August 10–16.

Name: _____ Grade: _____

Phone: _____ E-mail: _____

Schaumburg Township District Library

....

2009 Teen Summer Reading Program

The Fine Art of Reading
June 1–August 31

HOW TO PARTICIPATE

Fill out review slips for each book you read this summer. Use completed slips to "buy" prizes. While you can buy prizes in any order, only one each of the 3-, 5-, or 10-slip prizes will be available per teen.

BONUS DRAWINGS

Three drawings for $100 Woodfield Mall gift certificates will be held during the summer on the following dates: June 30, July 30, August 31. Slips used to purchase prizes all summer will be entered in the drawings. If teens have purchased all the prizes, they can still fill out more slips to add to the drawing entries.

1 slip:	Candy bar or granola bar
3 slips:	Mini art kit
5 slips:	Coupon for $5 off fines
10 slips:	$10 gift certificates to the library café (in $2 bills) for central library patrons or $10 to McDonald's for branch patrons

Schaumburg Township District Library
130 S. Roselle Rd. | Schaumburg, IL 60193 | (847) 985-4000 | www.stdl.org
Hoffman Estates Branch | 1550 Hassell Rd. | Hoffman Estates, IL 60169 | (847) 885-3511
Hanover Park Branch | 1266 Irving Park Rd. | Hanover Park, IL 60133 | (630) 372-7800

Schaumburg Township District Library

. . . .

2009 Teen Summer Reading Program

The Fine Art of Reading
June 1–August 31

PRIZE REDEMPTION SLIP

Name: _____ Grade: _____

E-mail address (if you want information on teen programs): _____

Title of book: _____

Three sentences about the book: _____

_____

_____

_____

Date redeemed: _____

Schaumburg Township District Library

....

2009 Summer Reading Program

The Fine Art of Reading
June 1–August 31

SUMMER READING REGISTRATION CARD

Last name, first name: _____

Library card #: _____ Phone: _____

1._____ Date redeemed: _____

2._____ Date redeemed: _____

3._____ Date redeemed: _____

4._____ Date redeemed: _____

5._____ Date redeemed:_____

Schaumburg Township District Library

....

Teen Appreciation Week

August 9–15

OVERDUE FINES COUPON: $10 OFF OVERDUE FINES

Name: _____ Grade: _____

Library card #: _____

May be used for overdues but not the cost of damaged materials. Teen patrons going into grades 6–12 may turn in one coupon only. It will be redeemable once from now until October 31, 2009.

Index

A

Abrahams, Peter, *Down the Rabbit Hole,* 22
activities
    autobiography, 13
    book trailers, 12
    collages as activities, 5
    college finance activities, 9
    comfort items, creating activities, 7
    Community Collaborations (program), 7–8,
        103–106
    CREATEen (club), 5
    credit, caution using, 9
    film activities, promotional, 11
    fund and food raising, 7
    game night, 10
    improv, 11
    lighting and mood design, 12
    Money Mavericks (club), 9
    musical chairs with ringtones, 10
    promotional video, 13
    puzzles and passive, 33–43
    savings board, 9
    scholarship and grant search, 9
    Techno Teens (club), 10–11
    Telling Stories with Film (club), 12–13
    texting, speed, 10
Adina, Shelley, *It's All about Us,* 27
The Adoration of Jenna Fox (Pearson), 31
after hours programs, 7
Alessio, Amy, 3, 87, 139–140
Alex Rider (book series), 36
All about Us (book series), 27
American Library Association (ALA), 19
Anderson, Laurie Halse, *Speak,* 26
Anime Viewers (program), 111, 113–114

April programs
    Battle of the Books, 74–75
    Poetry Slam, 75–76
    Primp Your Prom, 71–73
Art Media Mixer (program), 5, 97, 100–102
Art of Reading (booklist), 30
Asquith, Ros, *Yummy Stuff,* 32
Atwater-Rhodes, Amelia
    In the Forests of the Night, 26
    Persistence of Memory, 24
    Wolfcry, 29
auctions, 18
August programs
    Community Collaborations, 7–8, 103–106
    Library Orienteering, 103, 109–110
    Microwave Madness, 103, 106–108

B

Barnholdt, Lauren, *Two-Way Street,* 23
Battle of the Best (program), 47, 50–51
Battle of the Books (program), 74–75
Bauer, Cat, *Harley's Ninth,* 30
BBQ books (program), 97–98
Behind You (Woodson), 29
The Big Game of Everything (Lynch), 28
The Big Splash (Ferraiolo), 22
Bijlefeld, Marjolijn, *Food and You,* 32
Billingsley, Reshonda Tate, *Nothing but Drama,* 27
Blind Spot (Fabry), 27
Blue Bloods (de la Cruz), 24
booklists
    Art of Reading, 30
    Christian Fiction, 27
    Fabulous Food, 32

booklists (cont.)
Heartbreakers, 23
importance of, 21
Inspired Reads, 27
Mystery Madness, 22, 85, 87–93
Romance, 29
Science, 31
Short but Not Sweet, 26
Spending Savvy, 28
Vamping It Up, 24–25
booklogs, basic, 17–18
Booth, Coe, *Tyrell,* 28
Bucking the Sarge (Curtis), 28
Buffy the Vampire Slayer (book series), 36

C

Caine, Rachel, *Morganville Vampires,* 24
Carle, Megan, and Jill Carle, *Teens Cook,* 32
Carlson, Melody
New York Debut, 27
What Matters Most, 30
Carter House Girls (book series), 27
Cast, P. C., and Kristen Cast, *Marked,* 24
Catching Fire (Collins), 23
celebrations, teen reading, 19, 20, 147
A Certain Slant of Light (Whitcomb), 29
Charmed Life (book series), 27
Cheva, Cherry, *She's So Money,* 28
Christian Fiction (booklist), 27
Clique (book series), 27, 36
clubs
appeal of, 3
applications for, 8
CREATEens, 4–5
development of, 4–5, 8
Drama Dynamics, 11–12
feedback and adjustment of, 4
finance, 8–10
gauging success, 3
journaling, 47
Money Management, 8–10
Money Mavericks, 5
Techno Teen, 10–11
Telling Stories with Film, 12–13
themed, 4–5
volunteering, 7–8
writing, 47
See also programs
Cohn, Rachel, *Cupcake,* 32
Colasanti, Susane, *Waiting for You,* 23
Collins, Nancy, *Vamps,* 24
Collins, Suzanne, *Catching Fire,* 23
comic contest, 111–113, 143
Community Collaborations (program), 7–8, 103–106

contests
comic, 111, 143
Dream Rooms Design, 133, 135–136
Mangamania Reviewing, 117, 120–121
songwriting, 99–100
Stellar Scene, 125–127
crafts, edible, 6
CREATEen (club), 4–6
Creative Carding (program), 125, 127–129
The Crossroads (Grabenstein), 22
Cupcake (Cohn), 32
Curtis, Christopher Paul, *Bucking the Sarge,* 28
Cyd Charisse Trilogy (book series), 32

D

The Dangerous Days of Daniel X (Patterson and Ledwidge), 31
Dayton, Anne, *The Miracle Girls* (Vanderbilt), 27
de la Cruz. Melissa, *Blue Bloods,* 24
The Dead and Gone (Pfeffer), 31
Dead Girls Don't Write Letters (Giles), 26
December programs
Decked-Out Halls, 133, 137
Dream Rooms Design contest, 133, 135–136
Festival of Cultures, 133, 134
Decked-Out Halls (program), 133, 137
digital crafting, 5
Diver, Lucienne, *Vamped,* 24
Divine (book series), 27
Doctorow, Cory, *Little Brother,* 31
Dopple Ganger Chronicles (book series), 22
Dowd, Siobhan, *The London Eye Mystery,* 22
Down the Rabbit Hole (Abrahams), 22
Drama Dynamics (club), 11–12
Dramarama (Lockhart), 30
Draper, Sharon, *Tears of a Tiger,* 26
Dream Rooms Design Contest, 133, 135–136

E

Echo Falls Mystery (book series), 22
events, drop-in, 8
Evermore (Noel), 25, 29
Evernight (Gray), 24
Everyone Reads (program), 20
Exercentral (worksheet), 38

F

Fabry, Chris, *Blind Spot,* 27
Fabulous Food (booklist), 32
February programs
Oscar-Style Teen Film Fest, 55–57
Social Networking Safety Net, 55, 60–62
Wild Hearts Charm Bracelets, 55, 58–59
Ferraiolo, Jack D., *The Big Splash,* 22
Festival of Cultures (program), 133, 134
Film (club). *see* Telling Stories with Film (club)
Finance (club), 8–10
The First Escape (Taylor), 22
The First Part Last (Johnson), 26
Flake, Sharon, *Money Hungry,* 28
Food and You (Bijlefeld), 32
Found (Haddix), 22
Franklin, Emily, *The Other Half of Me,* 30
Friendship Fest, 63–66

G

Garage Band (Gipi), 30
Get a Clue in the Library, 85, 94–96
Getting the Girl (Juby), 32
Giles, Gail, *Dead Girls Don't Write Letters,* 26
Gipi, *Garage Band,* 30
Glamour Tools (worksheet), 43
Godbersen, Anna, *The Luxe,* 23
Gone (Grant), 31
Good Girlz (book series), 27
Gossip Girl (book series), 36
Grabenstein, Chris, *The Crossroads,* 22
Grant, Michael, *Gone,* 31
Gray, Claudia, *Evernight,* 24
Green, John
Looking for Alaska, 23
Paper Towns, 22

H

Haddix, Margaret Peterson, *Found,* 22
Harley's Ninth (Bauer), 30
Harrison, Lisi, *Massie,* 28
Hartinger, Brent, *Project Sweet Life,* 28
Hattori, Chihiro, *The Manga Cookbook,* 32
The Haunted (book series), 22
Haunted Gingerbread Houses (program), 117, 122–123
Heartbreaker (booklist), 23
Henderson, Lauren, *Kiss Me Kill Me,* 22
Holbrook, Lauren (book series), 27
Holiday History (worksheet), 39

Hollywood Nobody (Samson), 27
Hollywood Nobody (book series), 27
The Host (Meyer), 31
House of Dance (Kephart), 30
House of Night (book series), 24
How Will It End? (worksheet), 35

I

I Heart You (Schroeder), 29
If You Come Softly (Woodson), 26
The Immortals (book series), 25, 29
In the Forests of the Night (Atwater-Rhodes), 26
Inspired Reads (booklist), 27
It's All about Us (Adina), 27

J

January programs
    Battle of the Best, 47, 50–51
    Start the Year Out Write!, 47–49
    Wii Are Fit, 47, 52–53
Jenkins, A. M., *Night Road*, 24
Jinks, Catherine, *The Reformed Vampire Support Group*, 22, 24
Job Skills for Successful Teens, 80–82
Johnson, Angela, *The First Part Last*, 26
Jones, Jenny B., *So Not Happening*, 27
journaling, clubs, 47
Juby, Susan, *Getting the Girl*, 32
July programs
    Art Media Mixer, 5, 97, 100–102
    BBQ Books, 97–98
    songwriting contest, 99–100
June programs
    Get a Clue in the Library, 85, 94–96
    Mystery Madness, 22, 85, 87–93
    Techno Book Discussions, 85–87

K

Kansas City Public Library, 19
Kephart, Beth, *House of Dance*, 30
Kiss Me Kill Me (Henderson), 22
Kissing Coffins (Schreiber), 26
Krizmanic, Judy, *The Teen's Vegetarian Cookbook*, 32

L

Lauren Holbrook (book series), 27
Ledwidge, Michael, *The Dangerous Days of Daniel X* (Patterson), 31
Library Orienteering, 103, 109–110
The Life of Angelica Cookson Potts (book series), 32
Little Brother (Doctorow), 31

Little Known Library Facts (worksheet), 34
Living Dead Girl (Scott), 26
Lockhart, E., *Dramarama*, 30
The London Eye Mystery (Dowd), 22
Looking for Alaska (Green), 23
Lucky (Vail), 28
The Luxe (Godbersen), 23
Lynch, Chris, *The Big Game of Everything*, 28

M

Magic Moment Writing Challenge, 77–80
The Manga Cookbook (Hattori), 32
Manga Match (worksheet), 41
Mangamania Reviewing contest, 117, 120–121
Mangum, Erynn, *Miss Match*, 27
March Madness Basketball and Books, 66–67
March programs
    Friendship Fest, 63–66
    March Madness Basketball and Books, 66–67
    Totally Tech Lock-in, 63, 68–70
Marked (Cast and Cast), 24
Marr, Melissa, *Wicked Lovely*, 29
Massie (Harrison), 28
Maximum Ride (book series), 36
May Programs
    Job Skills for Successful Teens, 80–82
    Magic Moment Writing Challenge, 77–80
    Summer Reading Kickoff, 83–84
McDonald, Janet, *Spellbound*, 26
McMann, Lisa, *Wake*, 29
Mead, Richelle, *Vampire Academy*, 25
Meehl, Brian, *Suck It Up*, 25
Menu Selections (worksheet), 37
Meyer, Stephenie, *The Host*, 31
Microwave Madness (program), 103, 106–108
The Miracle Girls (Dayton and Vanderbilt), 27
Miss Match (Mangum), 27
The Missing (book series), 22
Money Hungry (Flake), 28
Money Management (club), 8–10
Money Mavericks (club), 5, 8–10
Moneyene (program), 8, 125, 129–131
Morganville Vampires (Caine), 24
My Cup Runneth Over (Whytock), 32
Mystery Madness, 22, 85, 87–93
Mystery Madness (booklist), 22, 85, 87–93

N

New Teen Titans (book series), 36
New York Debut (Carlson), 27
The Night My Sister Went Missing (Plum-Ucci), 22
Night Road (Jenkins), 24
Noel, Alyson, *Evermore*, 25, 29
Nothing but Drama (Billingsley), 27
November programs
    Creative Carding, 125, 127–129
    Moneyene, 8, 125, 129–131
    Stellar Scene contest, 125–127

O

October programs
    Haunted Gingerbread Houses, 117, 122–123
    Mangamania Reviewing contest, 117, 120–121
    Totally Teen Read-in, 118–119
One Community Book (program), 16, 20
Oscar-Style Teen Film Fest, 55–57
The Other Half of Me (Franklin), 30

P

painting, power, 6
Paper Towns (Green), 22
Patterson, James, *The Dangerous Days of Daniel X* (Ledwidge), 31
Patton, Kim, 3, 87, 139–140
Pauley, Kimberly, *Sucks to Be Me*, 25
Pearson, Mary, *The Adoration of Jenna Fox*, 31
Persistence of Memory (Atwater-Rhodes), 24
Pfeffer, Susan, *The Dead and Gone*, 31
Plum-Ucci, Carol, *The Night My Sister Went Missing*, 22
Poetry Slam (program), 75–76
Primp Your Prom (program), 71–73
prizes, stepped, 18
programs
    age range for, 46
    Anime Viewers, 111, 113–114
    Art Media Mixer, 5, 97, 100–102
    Battle of the Best, 47, 50–51
    BBQ books, 97–98
    Community Collaborations, 7–8, 103–106
    Creative Carding, 125, 127–129
    Decked-Out Halls, 133, 137
    Everyone Reads, 20
    Festival of Cultures, 133, 134
    Friendship Fest, 63–66
    Get a Clue in the Library, 85, 94–96
    Haunted Gingerbread Houses, 117, 122–123

programs (cont.)
    Job Skills for Successful Teens, 80–82
    length of time for, 45
    Library Orienteering, 103, 109–110
    Magic Moment Writing Challenge, 77–80
    Microwave Madness, 103, 106–108
    Moneyene, 8, 125, 129–131
    Mystery Madness, 22, 85, 87–93
    order of events for, 46
    Oscar-Style Teen Film Fest, 55–57
    participant numbers for, 45
    Poetry Slam, 75–76
    preparation time for, 45
    Primp Your Prom, 71–73
    promotion of, 46
    Science Fair Fun, 111, 115–116
    setting up of, 46
    shopping suggestions for, 46
    Social Networking Safety Net, 55, 60–62
    Start the Year Out Write!, 47–49
    Techno Book Discussions, 85–87
    Totally Tech Lock-in, 63, 68–70
    variations in, 46
    Wii Are Fit, 47, 52–53
    Wild Hearts Charm Bracelets, 55, 58–59
    See also reading programs
Project Sweet Life (Hartinger), 28
Prom Dress Exchange, 71

R
Raven (Van Diepen), 29
reading programs
    Battle of the Books, 74–75
    booklogs, 17–18
    goals of, 15–16
    Mangamania Reviewing Contest, 117, 120–121
    March Madness Basketball and Books, 66–67
    summer, 17–18, 144–146
    Summer Reading Kickoff, 83–84
    teen celebrations of, 19
    Totally Teen Read-In, 118–119
    winter, 17–18, 144–146
    year round, 19
A Really Nice Prom Mess (Sloan), 23
The Reformed Vampire Support Group (Jinks), 22, 24
Rider, Alex (book series), 36
ringtones
    musical chairs and, 10
    name that ringer, 11
Romance (booklist), 29
RPM (book series), 27

S
Sachar, Louis, *Small Steps,* 28
Samson, Lisa, *Hollywood Nobody,* 27
Scarlett Wakefield (book series), 22
Schaumburg Township District Library, 8, 16, 139
Schreiber, Ellen, *Kissing Coffins,* 26
Schreiber, Ellen, *Vampire Kisses,* 25
Schroeder, Lisa, *I Heart You,* 29
Science (booklist), 31
Science Fair Fun, 111, 115–116
Scott, Elizabeth, *Living Dead Girl,* 26
September programs
    Anime Viewers, 111, 113–114
    Comic contest, 111–113, 143
    Science Fair Fun, 111, 115–116
Shapeshifter (book series), 29
She's So Money (Cheva), 28
Short but Not Sweet (booklist), 26
Shusterman, Neal, *Unwind,* 31
Simply Divine (Thomas), 27
Sloan, Brian, *A Really Nice Prom Mess,* 23
Small Steps (Sachar), 28
Smith, Cynthia Leitich, *Tantalize,* 29
Smith, L. J., *Vampire Diaries,* 25
So Not Happening (Jones), 27
Social Networking Safety Net, 55, 60–62
Sookie Stackhouse (book series), 36
Songwriting contest, 99–100
Sonnenblick, Jordan, *Zen and the Art of Faking It,* 30
Speak (Anderson), 26
Spellbound (McDonald), 26
Spending Savvy (booklist), 28
The Spring of Candy Apples (Viguia), 27
Stackhouse, Sookie (book series), 36
Start the Year Off Write! (program), 47–49
Stellar Scene contest, 125–127
Stern, Sam, *The Teen Survival Cookbook,* 32
Story of a Girl (Zarr), 30
Stuck in Neutral (Trueman), 26
Suck It Up (Meehl), 25
Sucks to Be Me (Pauley), 25
Summer Reading Kickoff, 83–84
summer reading programs, 17–18, 144–146
The Sweet Life of Stella Madison (Zieses), 32
Sweet Seasons (book series), 27

T
Tantalize (Smith), 29
Taylor, G.P., *The First Escape,* 22
Tears of a Tiger (Draper), 26
Techno Book Discussion, 85–87

Techno Teens (club), 10–11
Teen Appreciation Week, 147
Teen Corps, 8, 142
Teen Read Week, 19, 111, 117
The Teen Survival Cookbook (Stern), 32
Teen Tech Week, 63
Teens Cook (Carle and Carle), 32
The Teen's Vegetarian Cookbook (Krizmanic), 32
Telling Stories with Film (club), 12–13
Thomas, Jacquelin, *Simply Divine,* 27
Totally Tech Lock-in, 63, 68–70
Totally Teen Read-In, 118–119
Trueman, Terry, *Stuck in Neutral,* 26
Twilight (book series), 29, 36
Two-Way Street (Barnholdt), 23
Tyrell (Booth), 28

U
The Uglies (Westerfeld), 31
Uncanny X Men (book series), 36
Unwind (Shusterman), 31

V
Vail, Rachel, *Lucky,* 28
Vamped (Diver), 24
Vamping It Up (booklist), 24–25
Vampire Academy (Mead), 25
Vampire Diaries (Smith), 25
Vampire Kisses (Schreiber), 25
Vampire Kisses (book series), 25, 26, 29
Vamps (Collins), 24
Van Diepen, Allison, *Raven,* 29
Vanderbilt, May, *The Miracle Girls* (Dayton), 27
Vegetable Variety (worksheet), 40
videos, promotional, 13
Viguia, Debbie, *The Spring of Candy Apples,* 27
Virtual Teen Advisory Board, 4
Volunteering and Community Partnerships (program), 7–8
volunteering needs, immediacy, 7

W
Waiting for You (Colasanti), 23
Wake (McMann), 29
Wakefield, Scarlett (book series), 22
Westerfeld, Scott, *The Uglies,* 31
What Matters Most (Carlson), 30
Whitcomb, Laura, *A Certain Slant of Light,* 29
Whose Team Are You On? (worksheet), 36
Whytock, Cherry, *My Cup Runneth Over,* 32
Wicked Lovely (Marr), 29

Wicked Lovely (book series), 29
Wii Are Fit (program), 47, 52–53
Wild Hearts Charm Bracelets (class), 55, 58–59
winter reading programs, 17–18, 47
Wolfcry (Atwater-Rhodes), 29
Woodson, Jackie, *If You Come Softly,* 26
Woodson, Jacqueline, *Behind You,* 29
worksheets
    Exercentral, 38
    Glamour Tools, 43
    Holiday History, 39
    How Will It End?, 35
    Little Known Library Facts, 34
    Manga Match, 41
    Menu Selections, 37
    Vegetable Variety, 40
    Whose Team Are You On?, 36
    Worst Ending in Films, 42
Worst Ending in Films (worksheet), 42
writing, clubs, 47

Y

A Year of Programs for Teens (Alessio and Patton), 3, 87

year-round programs, 19
Young Adult Library Services Association (YALSA), 19
Yummy Stuff (Asquith), 32

Z

Zarr, Sara, *Story of a Girl,* 30
Zen and the Art of Faking It (Sonnenblick), 30
Zieses, Lara M, *The Sweet Life of Stella Madison,* 32

You may also be interested in

YOUNG ADULT LITERATURE
FROM ROMANCE TO REALISM

Michael Cart

Today's young adult literature is every bit as complex as the audience it's written for, unflinchingly addressing such topics as homosexuality, mental illness, AIDS, and drug abuse. In this much expanded revision of his 1996 book, Cart shows how the best of contemporary YA lit has evolved to tackle such daunting subjects without resorting to sensationalism.

PRINT: 978-0-8389-1045-0
EBOOK: 7400-0450
PRINT/EBOOK BUNDLE: 7700-0450
256 PGS / 6" × 9"

A YEAR OF PROGRAMS FOR TEENS
AMY J. ALESSIO AND KIMBERLY A. PATTON
ISBN: 978-0-8389-0903-4

THE HIPSTER LIBRARIAN'S GUIDE TO TEEN CRAFT PROJECTS
TINA COLEMAN AND PEGGIE LLANES
ISBN: 978-0-8389-0971-3

DESIGNING SPACE FOR CHILDREN AND TEENS IN LIBRARIES AND PUBLIC PLACES
SANDRA FEINBERG AND JAMES R. KELLER, AIA
ISBN: 978-0-8389-1020-7

YOUNG ADULTS DESERVE THE BEST
SARAH FLOWERS FOR YALSA
ISBN: 978-0-8389-3587-3

QUICK AND POPULAR READS FOR TEENS
EDITED BY PAM SPENCER HOLLEY FOR YALSA
ISBN: 978-0-8389-3577-4

RISKY BUSINESS
LINDA W. BRAUN, HILLIAS J. MARTIN, AND CONNIE URQUHART FOR YALSA
ISBN: 978-0-8389-3596-5

Order today at **alastore.ala.org** or **866-746-7252!**

ALA Store purchases fund advocacy, awareness, and accreditation programs for library professionals worldwide.